10/6

Rediscovering
the I Ching

Greg Whincup

Rediscovering the I Ching

DOUBLEDAY & COMPANY, INC., GARDEN CITY, NEW YORK
1986

Caligraphy by *South China Arts, Victoria, B.C.*

Library of Congress Cataloging-in-Publication Data
Whincup, Gregory.
    Rediscovering the I Ching.
    Bibliography: p.
    1. I ching.   I. Title.
PL2464.Z7W46   1986   299'.51282   85-20595
ISBN 0-385-19667-9

*This book is dedicated to the memory
of my mother, Doreen Scrivener Whincup.*

PREFACE

Over the past hundred years, several translations of the ancient Chinese *I Ching* or *Book of Changes* have been written. These differ in various ways, but all of them are based on the same traditional ideas of what the *Changes* means. The present translation is something new. It follows modern Chinese scholars back to a time before the traditional interpretations were formed and attempts to rediscover the original meaning of the *Changes*.

The *Changes* was written as a divination manual, a book of power. Ancient soothsayers used it to predict the outcome of their patrons' plans. Later commentators, however, came to view it as a book of philosophy as well, reinterpreting it in metaphysical and moral terms.

The *Changes* was written almost three thousand years ago, during the Chinese Bronze Age. It was not until several centuries later that the first great commentaries laid down the interpretations of the text that became traditional in China. By this time, the *Changes'* archaic language had already become difficult to understand and Chinese thought had become much more sophisticated. The commentators reinterpreted the text in terms of their own philosophical systems. They turned it from a simple divination handbook into a philosophical work that expresses moral and metaphysical truths in the form of divinations.

Only in the twentieth century have Chinese scholars begun to get a better historical perspective on the *Changes*. Knowledge of ancient China has improved by leaps and bounds as a result of archaeological discoveries and better methods of scholarship. New studies reveal a *Changes* very different both in tone and in substance from the one handed down by tradition. Rather than making general moral points and stressing moral improvement, it is a pragmatic manual of divination that tells ambitious feudal noblemen how to deal with concrete situations in their lives. It is less philosophically profound than the traditional *Changes*, but much more straightforward.

My aim in *Rediscovering the I Ching* has been to rediscover this original *Changes* and to present it clearly for the modern reader. In the translation itself, I have tried to convey the poetical and mantic quality of the Chinese text while still making its meaning clear. Though I lean heavily on the work of modern Chinese scholars, some of the interpretations are my own. In explanatory notes, I try to clarify the text's meaning, in part by relating it to the overall symbolic pattern of the *Changes*. To do this, I introduce some new ideas about the *Changes'* symbolism.

The basis of the *Changes* is a set of sixty-four six-line diagrams called "hexagrams" (e.g., ☰ , ☷ , ☶ , ☵). Each hexagram and each line has a symbolic meaning that the text is there to describe. The question is, why does a hexagram or line mean what the text says it does? Traditional explanations often seem forced. This translation presents new explanations based on simple and more coherent patterns of symbolism. These patterns are described on pages 3 to 6. While they do not explain everything, they make up a framework within which the inner logic of the hexagrams becomes apparent.

No one will ever rediscover exactly what the *Changes'* authors intended it to mean. For one thing, numerous errors are known to have been transcribed into the text and not all of them can be corrected. For another, the text's almost telegraphic conciseness makes some passages ambiguous or entirely obscure. To this extent, this new translation is one more in a long line of personal versions of the *Changes* that have been written in China and abroad over the last two millennia. Hopefully it is a version that will bring the modern Western reader closer to the original *Changes* than he or she has yet been able to go.

I would like to thank Professor Catherine Stevens and Dr. Hsio-Yen Shih for keeping me in the field of Chinese studies; Dr. Chin-hsiung Hsu for introducing me to Bronze Age China; Dave Gunn for sparking my interest in the *Changes*; Mr. Francis Naish for his many kindnesses; and Sheila, for everything.

Greg Whincup

Sooke, Vancouver Island
April 1985

CONTENTS

Rediscovering
the I Ching

INTRODUCTION

The first people to use the *Changes* were priestly diviners serving the feudal lords of the Bronze Age Zhou Dynasty in China, sometime between about 1000 and 500 B.C.

The heart of the book is a set of sixty-four diagrams called "hexagrams," each of which symbolizes a different human situation. The text consists of passages that describe the symbolic meanings of the hexagrams.

In making a divination, the diviner selected a hexagram at random and took it as a symbol of the situation about which he had been asked. Supernatural forces were believed to govern this apparently random choice of a hexagram.

The sixty-four hexagrams are every possible combination of six solid (——) and/or broken (—— ——) horizontal lines placed one above the other. The symbolic meanings of the hexagrams are based on seeing solid lines as strong and active and broken lines as weak and acquiescent, e.g., QIÁN ☰ STRONG ACTION, KŪN ☷ ACQUIESCENCE, GÒU ☴ SUBJUGATED.

No one knows the origins of the *Changes*. Estimates of its date range from as early as before 1100 B.C. to as late as after 400 B.C. Some scholars believe that it was written by one man, others that it is a compilation of the work of many.

My own tentative hypothesis is that the text was compiled over a period between about 1000 and 500 B.C. as the handbook of a school of diviners; that it contains material dating from at least the beginning of this period; and that it was probably largely complete by about 700 B.C.

The *Changes* was written under the Zhou Dynasty, which came to power shortly before 1000 B.C. and retained nominal power until about 250 B.C. The Zhou were China's second Bronze Age dynasty, succeeding the powerful Shang who had conquered and unified the Stone Age farming hamlets of north China in about 1750 B.C.

The Zhou people had their origins on the western borders of the Shang empire. Two successive lords of Zhou rose to be important Shang nobles, commanders of the western region of the empire. It was their successor who finally led a rebellion against Shang, defeated it, and established his own dynasty.

The Zhou justified their rebellion on the grounds of Shang extravagance, licentiousness, and cruelty, contrasting these faults with their own frugality, uprightness, and concern for people's welfare.

The text of the *Changes* mentions a number of historical events connected with the Zhou conquest of Shang. In fact, the entire text appears to be loosely based on the Zhou rise to power, with its hexagrams arranged to follow a minor nobleman's rise from obscurity to eminence to supreme power.

In Bronze Age China, an aristocracy of large and small landholders lived off what slaves, serfs, and/or free peasants produced from the land. Under Zhou, these noblemen appear to have been more independent than they were under Shang and the Zhou king gradually lost power to his great nobles, who became rulers of what were virtually independent states. Between about 750 and 250 B.C., the greater nobles swallowed up the lesser and the history of China became one of increasingly bloody warfare among a decreasing number of larger and larger states.

Ancient histories indicate that diviners used the *Changes* to advise rulers of the time on matters of war, marriage, and succession. In the histories, the book is called either the *Changes* (易 *Yì*) or the *Changes of Zhou* (周易 *Zhōu Yì*).

The chaotic final centuries of the Zhou period spawned the first golden age of Chinese philosophy. Then and during the more orderly Han period that followed, the *Changes* came to be seen as a book of ethics and metaphysics as well as one of divination. A number of commentaries were written that reinterpreted the *Changes* in this light and expounded on its symbolism and philosophical significance.

Several of these commentaries were put together with the basic text of the *Changes* to make up the *Classic of Change* or *I Ching* (易經 *Yìjīng*). This has been the basis of *Changes* interpretation for the past two thousand years.

Coupled with errors that had already been made in the transcription of the text itself, the commentaries obscured the rather simpler original meaning of the *Changes*. Modern archaeology and historical and philological scholarship in China have now made it possible to rediscover some of that original meaning.

THE SYMBOL SYSTEM
OF THE *CHANGES*

The basis of the *Changes* is a set of sixty-four six-line diagrams called "hexagrams," e.g., ☰☰ , ☰☰ . Each of these symbolizes a different human situation and each of a hexagram's six lines symbolizes a different stage or aspect of that situation.

There is a passage of text to explain and illustrate the symbolic meaning of each hexagram and separate passages for each one of its lines.

The symbolism of the *Changes* is based on seeing solid lines (——) as strong, solid, and active and broken lines (— —) as weak, inactive, receptive, and acquiescent. The meanings of all the hexagrams are ultimately derived from this simple symbolism.

The eight trigrams Each hexagram can be analyzed into an upper group of three lines and a lower group of three lines. These are called the upper and lower "trigrams."

There are eight different trigrams and each of them has a specific symbolic meaning based on its arrangement of solid and broken lines. For example, ☱ means to kneel in submission, perhaps because it shows someone weak (— —) kneeling under someone very strong (☰).

The meanings of most of the hexagrams are based on those of their component trigrams. For instance, ☱ Kneel in Submission under ☰ Strong Action gives the hexagram ☰☱ SUBJUGATED, in which one kneels in submission to someone overwhelmingly strong. And ☰ Strong Action under ☷ Acquiescent gives the hexagram ☷☰ FLOWING, in which someone in a low position advances strongly, without resistance from someone in a higher position.

It was only because such derivations are almost universally possible that I came to believe the trigrams were indeed part of the *Changes'* original symbol system. Since the text never directly mentions the trigrams, the possibility existed that they were a category invented by later commentators, where early diviners saw only the hexagrams and their individual lines.

In fact, there are only a few hexagrams whose meaning can be derived in any other way, e.g., ䷖ DESTRUCTION, where one lies on a high couch (the solid top line ——) whose weak supports (the five weak lines below it ☷) are cut away.

Here are the meanings of the eight trigrams, along with ways in which those meanings can be related to the trigrams' structure:

☰ 乾 Qián   Strong Action (active, solid, strong): three strong and active solid lines.

☷ 巛 Kūn   Acquiescent (passive, obedient, weak, inert, accepting, a crowd): three weak and passive broken lines.

☵ 坎 Kǎn   Pit (trouble, danger, difficulties, a river to be forded): The solid line is like solid ground, with gaping pits either side of it.

☲ 離 Luó   Shining Light (shining, shone upon, within): The broken line is a weak subject, surrounded by the shining glory of a strong ruler represented by the two solid lines.

☳ 震 Zhèn   Thunderbolt (rush forward, a burst of motion): A strong line rushes forward through two weak lines, its strength gradually fading away.

☶ 艮 Gēn   Keep Still (stop, stopped, restraint): A solid line blocks the advance of two broken lines, which are passive in any case.

☴ 巽 Xùn   Kneel in Submission (submit to, unite with): A weak line kneels beneath two strong lines.

☱ 兌 Duì   Stand Straight (break free, step forward): *Either* two strong lines stand up through the opening provided by a weak line *or* a weak line breaks free from two strong lines.

The meanings given to the trigrams here differ somewhat from those given to them traditionally and in other translations. That is because they are derived entirely from my interpretation of the text itself, without reference to later commentaries. The meanings of the trigrams can be inferred from those of the eight hexagrams formed by reduplicating one of the eight trigrams, e.g., ䷹ STAND STRAIGHT, and also from the ways in which the various trigrams combine to form other hexagrams.

The six lines Each of the six lines of a hexagram symbolizes a different stage or aspect of the situation symbolized by the hexagram as a whole. Moreover each of the six possible positions in a hexagram has a characteristic range of meaning: all first lines are similar, all fifth lines are similar, and so on.

1. first line — This bottom line is associated with low social position, smallness, feet, and an animal's tail. It often has to do with beginning something or with the earliest stages of a situation.

2. line two — This is the place of the subject or subordinate. Since it is right in the middle of the lower trigram, which is considered the inner trigram, it sometimes has to do with being inside something. It is also associated with women, who spent much of their time within the home.

3. line three — Line three is the place of danger and difficulties. Coming at the top of the lower trigram, it often shows the misfortunes that befall someone who attempts to rise above his proper station and make the dangerous crossing to the upper trigram.

4. line four — This is the place of the officer, someone who is in a high position (the upper trigram) but below the ruler (line five). Since it is the first line of the upper trigram, it symbolizes entry into high position. It often shows a successful resolution of difficulties encountered in line three.

5. line five — Line five is the place of the ruler. It is usually a hexagram's most auspicious line. Just as the line of the subject is in the middle of the lower trigram, the line of the ruler is in the middle of the upper trigram.

6. top line — This line usually has to do with going too far, or reaching too high. Since it is above the line of the ruler, it often describes the conflict that results when a subject places himself above his ruler. Coming at the end of the hexagram, it sometimes shows the end of one general situation and the beginning of another.

The symbol system of the *Changes* is not so strictly systematic that only one meaning is possible for each hexagram or line. Of several possible meanings, the *Changes'* authors judged one appropriate and composed the text on that basis.

The sequence Not only are there patterns in the structure of each hexagram, there is also a pattern in the sequence of the sixty-four hexagrams. This follows a nobleman's rise from obscurity and weakness to a position of great power. It appears to be loosely based on the rise of the lord of Zhou from chief of an obscure western tribe to king of all China.

The story starts with QIÁN (1) STRONG ACTION and its protagonist goes through several cycles of advance and retreat, allegiance and dissatisfaction, subordination and independence, gradually increasing in power. He reaches the height of power in GÉ (49) REVOLUTION, where he overthrows the king, and DǏNG (50) THE RITUAL CALDRON, where he establishes his own regime. The final fourteen hexagrams, from ZHÈN (51) THUNDER-BOLTS to WÈI JÌ (64) NOT YET ACROSS, follow a new protagonist, a vassal of the conquered king, as he finds a place in the new order and then begins his own advance. A complete outline of the sequence appears as Appendix A.

The pattern of the sequence is far from strict. Some hexagrams fit it less well than others. But one sequential pattern is strictly followed: All the hexagrams are arranged in pairs both by structure and by meaning. Every hexagram is either the inverse or the reverse of its mate: It is either its mate turned upside down (e.g., number 3 ䷂ and number 4 ䷃) or with solid and broken lines reversed (e.g., number 1 ䷀ and number 2 ䷁). Most pairs are inverse pairs; only four are reverse pairs.

This structural pattern is reflected in the hexagrams' meanings as well. Every hexagram is in some sense the opposite of its mate. Among the clearest illustrations of this are QIÁN (1) STRONG ACTION and KŪN (2) ACQUIESCENCE. Less obvious are TÚN (3) GATHERING SUPPORT and MÉNG (4) THE YOUNG SHOOT. The protagonist of GATHERING SUPPORT is someone weak who restrains himself from advancing until he has gathered support. That of THE YOUNG SHOOT advances recklessly but is restrained by someone else.

DIVINATION WITH THE *CHANGES*

There were two main methods of divination in ancient China: oracle bone divination and yarrow divination. The *Changes* is a handbook of yarrow divination.

Oracle bone or "tortoise" divination was used by the Shang kings and remained the most prestigious method even under Zhou, when yarrow divination was more widely used. Diviners read omens in the cracks that sprouted when a specially prepared tortoise shell or shoulder blade of an ox was heated with a red-hot poker. From the ruins of the Shang capital archaeologists have unearthed a treasure trove of bones and shells inscribed with divinations made for the ancient kings.

In yarrow divination, the stiff stalks of the common yarrow or milfoil plant were used. Diviners constructed a hexagram on the basis of random sorting of a number of yarrow stalks.

The earliest surviving outline of their method dates from sometime during the last couple of centuries B.C. This says that the diviner took 49 yarrow stalks, divided them at random into two piles, then counted through each pile by fours, discarding the eventual remainders. He combined the piles and repeated this process twice more, until there were exactly 6, 7, 8, or 9 groups of four stalks each left (i.e., 24, 28, 32, or 36 stalks).

This number determined whether the bottom line of the hexagram would be a solid line (7 ——), a broken line (8 — —), a solid line changing to a broken line (9 —→ — —), or a broken line changing to a solid line (6 — → ——). The entire procedure was repeated to obtain each of the six lines of the answering hexagram.

In general, if the hexagram was all stable 7 and 8 lines, the hexagram as a whole was the answer to the divination. If there was one changing 6 or 9 line, that line was the answer. And if more than one line changed, a new hexagram was formed by changing those lines and the two hexagrams together were the answer.

For example, the hexagram KÙN (47) BURDENED:

```
8  — —    BURDENED. He who is burdened will be blessed. It is
7  ——              auspicious for a big man to persevere,
7  ——              he will come to no harm. Words spoken
8  — —             against him will not be believed.
7  ——
8  — —
```

A nobleman who received this in divination would have been confident about persevering in the face of difficulties.

But what if line three were a 6 instead of an 8? Then, because it was a changing line, line three would be the answer to the divination:

```
8  — —    BURDENED
7  ——
7  ——
6  — →    line three — Weighed down by boulders, he leans for
7  ——              support on thorns. He enters his palace,
8  — —             but his wife is not there. Misfortune.
```

In this case, the same nobleman would have been less confident.

If several lines were changing lines, then the hexagram formed by changing them was taken together with the original hexagram as the answer:

```
BURDENED  6 — →   ——    INCREASE. It is favorable to
          7 ——    ——            advance. It is
          9 —→    — —           favorable to cross
          8 — —   — —           a great river.
          9 —→    — —
          6 — →   ——
```

Being burdened leads to increase. This answer would have encouraged the nobleman to persevere in any difficult undertaking.

For more detailed information about divination methods, see Appendix C. For some examples of ancient divinations, see Appendix B.

ANCIENT CHINA

The Stone Age Up until around 2000 B.C., a thousand years before the *Changes* was written, China was in the Stone Age. Separate neolithic tribes lived scattered through the plains, marshes, and woodlands of north China. Most of them were farmers, growing rice or millet in the river valleys. Wandering herdsmen and hunter-gatherers, however, still roamed the vast areas that remained uncultivated.

The farmers' material culture was quite advanced. Some produced fine wheel-formed pottery, had elegant highly polished stone tools, and made silk and other fabrics, which they sewed with bone needles. Most lived in circular thatch-roofed earthen huts with floors dug out a foot or two below ground level.

Chinese legend says this was the age of great emperors who began the irrigation and flood-control works that are characteristic of Chinese agriculture. Until recently, archaeologists had found no evidence of this. But now large ancient towns have been uncovered that some say are traces of the legendary first dynasty, the Xià 夏 (circa 2200–1750 B.C.).

The Shang Dynasty (circa 1750–1000 B.C.) The Shāng 商 people had their origins in the eastern part of north China. At first, they may have been vassals of the Xia, but they somehow gained possession of superior military technology — bronze weapons and the horse-drawn chariot — and swept westward, conquering the towns and villages of the north China plain.

The local farmers became serfs or slaves, supporting a Shang aristocracy with their production. The Shang clans kept a monopoly over bronze casting and used it to rule for over six centuries from fortified towns dotted around the countryside. In many ways, the dynasty is reminiscent of the great Bronze Age empires of Egypt and Mesopotamia.

The Shang reputation for cruelty and extravagance has been confirmed by modern archaeological excavations of their capital.

Interred in the tombs of the Shang kings were found literally hundreds of ritually slaughtered corpses, either offerings to the Shang gods or retinues for the dead kings.

On the other hand, the same excavations have revealed the high level of Shang culture. The well-developed writing system is a close ancestor of modern Chinese and Shang workshops produced what are technically and aesthetically some of the finest bronze objects ever made.

Shang's existence was only a legend until the beginning of this century, when it was spectacularly verified. Legend said that the village of Xiǎotún 小屯 in Henan province was near the site of the ancient Shang capital. Peasants of the village used to turn up strangely marked fragments of bone in their fields. They sold these to druggists, who called them "dragon bones" and pulverized them for use in various medicines.

Around the turn of the century, it was realized that the strange markings were a form of writing. By 1910 scholars had deciphered some of it and found that it recorded divinations made for the Shang kings over three thousand years before.

Just about anything the king planned to do was first put to the test of divination, allowing the spirits to pass judgment on it. The Shang method of divination is known in English as oracle bone divination and in Chinese as tortoise divination. Diviners read omens in the cracks that formed when a specially prepared tortoise shell or shoulder blade of an ox was heated with a red-hot poker. On the shell or bone, they recorded the question asked and sometimes the spirits' answer as well. Then they stored it away in underground archives, from which tens of thousands of inscribed fragments have now been recovered.

Among other things, the kings divined about war, hunting, sacrifice, and marriage and they made a regular divination on the fortune of the coming week. They offered sacrifice to a number of deities, principal among which were the Fathers and Mothers — the spirits of previous kings and queens. These were apparently believed to remain among men, determining the course of events. Some kings also sacrificed to deities associated with mountains, rivers, the sky, and the four directions.

When there was no war to occupy their energies, the king and his nobles devoted themselves to the hunt. Oracle records report many hunting expeditions, some of which netted enormous bags. On one royal hunt alone, the catch was 263 deer, 113 boars, and 10 rabbits. To eat meat was a privilege of the nobility.

In some of the oracle records, the name of a people called the

Zhōu 周 appears. In earlier examples, the king asks if he has the spirits' blessing for sending his Zhou vassals to attack his enemies. Later, however, he asks about sending other vassals to attack Zhou.

Such punitive raids were common and these would not be remarkable were it not for the fact that the Zhou were able to repel them and eventually attacked and overthrew Shang, establishing a new dynasty.

The Zhou Dynasty (circa 1000–250 B.C.) The Zhou tribe's homeland was in western China on the fringes of the Shang empire. Its own histories paint it as a rather backward nation of simple herdsmen and farmers. The Zhou saw themselves as possessors of ancient virtue, simpler and more upright than the luxurious Shang.

Under the next-to-last Shang king, Dìyǐ 帝乙, Chāng 昌, lord of Zhou, became one of the most important men in the empire, military commander of its western region. He was even given the oustanding honor of a bride from one of the royal clans.

But under Diyi's successor, Dìxīn 帝辛, this happy relationship came to an end. Chang was accused of treason and cast into prison for two years. According to one version of the story, he was not released until he had proven his loyalty by eating a stew made from his own eldest son.

As a border tribe, the Zhou had always been more independent than the noble clans in the center of the empire, but from this time on Zhou independence and power grew rapidly until Chang became the effective ruler of the western half of the empire. Despite his power, Chang made no open breach with Shang. It was not until twenty years after his death that his son Fā 發 attacked a place within the central region of the empire, in effect declaring war on Shang.

Two years later, Fa and the many allies who had rallied to the Zhou cause defeated Dixin's forces at the battle of Mùyě 牧野, only seventy-five kilometers (forty-five miles) from the Shang capital. Fa became the first king of the Zhou Dynasty, taking the title King Wu (武王 *Wǔwáng* "Martial King") and giving his father Chang the posthumous title King Wen (文王 *Wénwáng* "Gracious King").

The Zhou believed that their supreme deity Heaven had appointed them to punish Dixin for betraying the great traditions of earlier Shang rulers. They thought of Dixin as a degenerate who "took the advice of women and evil men,"[1] was cruel and extravagant, and drank to excess.

The truth of such propaganda is hard to determine. Certainly, both Diyi and Dixin were "unfamiliar with the virtues of moderation," as one Western scholar puts it.[2] Oracle records reveal that the scale of their hunts and sacrifices was particularly immense. Under

Zhou, the size of sacrifices was reduced and human sacrifice became almost unknown.

Under both Shang and Zhou, it was the custom for most of the food ostensibly prepared for sacrifice to the spirits actually to be eaten in a great feast following the ceremony. Under Shang, this was apparently the occasion for much drunkenness. Under Zhou, drunkenness was prohibited.

King Wu adopted a conciliatory policy toward supporters of the defeated Shang. He allowed many of them to keep the land they held from their former rulers and at the same time created a protective cordon by placing his own people on new fiefs in the empty land around and between them. Even the Shang crown prince Wǔgēng 武庚 was given land so that he could continue to propitiate the Fathers and Mothers. As a safeguard against him, however, three of King Wu's brothers were given fiefs around his.

A few years after the conquest, King Wu died. He was succeeded by his young son King Cheng (成王 Chéngwáng), but real power lay in the hands of a regent, the Duke of Zhou (周公 Zhōugōng), another brother of King Wu. The duke is remembered with kings Wen and Wu as one of the three great founders of the dynasty.

The Duke of Zhou was not universally popular at the time. Fearing the duke's power, Wugeng and the three Zhou brothers enfieffed around him rebelled together. The duke defeated them all and went on to lay a firm foundation for King Cheng and his successors. It is said that he made the country so peaceful and prosperous that criminal punishments were unnecessary throughout the reigns of King Cheng and his immediate successor, King Kang (康王 Kāng-wáng). This was the height of Zhou power.

Zhou society was organized in a kind of clan feudalism. The king nominally owned all the land, but he directly held only a small part of it. The rest he granted to his many nobles, most of whom were related to him in some way. The great nobles in turn granted small estates to their own subordinates. The fiefholder gave his lord military support, gifts of goods, and, most important of all, expressions of heartfelt loyalty and praise.

Despite the paramount importance of the king, he was not at the summit of the hierarchy — above him was Heaven, whom the Zhou conceived of as omnipotent ruler of the universe. Like the Shang, the Zhou venerated their ancestors with gifts of meat, wine, and grain, but they did not worship the other Shang deities.

As far as the common people were concerned, it is unclear whether the change of dynasties can have meant anything other than exchanging one set of masters for another. Most of the population worked the land as serfs, slaves, or small farmers (scholars are not agreed which) and even artisans and minor government officials could be awarded by the king as gifts to his nobles.

The division of the country into numerous semi-independent fiefs is the key to later Zhou history. Although these fiefs were nominally at the pleasure of the king, in practice they became hereditary. As time went by, the nobles with the largest fiefs became almost like rulers of independent states and the power of the king declined.

Shortly after 800 B.C., King You (幽王 *Yōuwáng*) fell in love with a beautiful young concubine called Bǎo Sì (褒姒) and deposed his empress and her son, the heir apparent, in favor of Bǎo Sì and her son. The empress's father, a great noble, helped an army of western nomads to invade the capital and kill the king. The capital, which was in the west of China, had to be abandoned to the invaders and the seat of government reestablished farther east, where the original heir apparent took office as King Ping (平王 *Píngwáng*).

The move to the east drastically reduced royal power. Much of the land that the kings had ruled directly lay in the west and was now lost. The royal holdings were reduced to those of a middle-ranking great noble. The king retained enormous prestige, but his wealth and power were gone. He became a pawn in the political maneuvers of the great states.

The shifting of the capital marks the end of the Western Zhou period (circa 1000–750 B.C.) and the beginning of the Eastern Zhou period (circa 750–250 B.C.), which is further divided into the Spring and Autumn period (circa 750–500 B.C.) and the Warring States period (circa 500–250 B.C.). Eastern Zhou was a time of increasingly violent warfare among a decreasing number of larger and larger states, as the more powerful states conquered and assimilated the weaker.

Up until shortly after 500 B.C., the states continued to be ruled by the families to whom they were given at the beginning of the dynasty. This period is called Spring and Autumn (春秋 *Chūnqiū*) after a history of it by that name. I believe that the *Changes* was written during Western Zhou and Spring and Autumn.

From 500 to 250 B.C., the disintegration of the old society accelerated and new ruling families took control of various states. This is called the Warring States period (戰國 *Zhànguó*) after another history, the *Stratagems of the Warring States* (戰國策 *Zhànguó Cè*).

The introduction of iron tools around 500 B.C. may have been an important factor in the disintegration of society. Bronze had always been too scarce and therefore prestigious a metal to be used in the fields; peasants apparently used stone tools throughout the Bronze Age. The appearance of iron tools increased production by making it possible for the same number of peasants to cultivate more land. Increased wealth led to the making of new fortunes and competition for the increased wealth led to two hundred and fifty years of staggeringly bloody warfare, made more bloody by the use of iron weapons and involving armies numbering into the hundreds of thousands.

The tribulations and social changes of the period stimulated China's first Golden Age of philosophy and scholarship. Many new schools of thought arose to try to make sense of the new world. Confucius, Mencius, Lao-tzu, and Chuang-tzu, among many others, lived during this time. All of Chinese culture, including the *Changes*, was reinterpreted and reevaluated.

The political chaos of Warring States came to an end in 221 B.C., when the ruler of a western state called Qin conquered all the other states and incorporated them into a united empire. This ruler — the First Qin Emperor (秦始皇 *Qín Shǐhuáng*) — not only put a stop to political disorder, he put a stop to disorder of all kinds. Weights and measures were standardized, the writing system was simplified and standardized, a network of post roads was built throughout the country, the defensive walls of the states were linked and extended to form the Great Wall of China, and political philosophies with which the emperor did not agree were banned.

A number of scholars were buried alive and objectionable books were burned, causing the loss to posterity of many important works. The *Changes* survived because practical books — those dealing with medicine, agriculture, and divination — were exempted from the ban.

The Qin Dynasty lasted only fifteen years. The First Emperor's brutality — and especially his cavalier treatment of many locally powerful people — meant that the less able Second Emperor had little base of support and fell within five years of his accession.

An ambitious adventurer called Líu Bāng (劉邦) gained the upper hand in the struggles that followed the end of the dynasty. In 206 B.C. he founded the glorious Han Dynasty, which kept China unified for four hundred years. During Han, a Confucian-based synthesis of the Warring States philosophies became China's dominant ideology. Patterns of government and culture were established that continued for two thousand years. The Chinese still call themselves the Han (漢).

THE HISTORY
OF THE *CHANGES*

No one can be sure when the *Changes* was written or by whom. Estimates of its date range from the time of the Zhou conquest of Shang before 1000 B.C., all the way up to the Warring States period after 500 B.C. Some scholars believe it was the work of one man, others that it is a compilation of the work of many. There are good arguments on all sides, but none of them is conclusive.[3]

In traditional China, it was agreed that the *Changes'* text dated from the time of the conquest. During the time he was imprisoned by the Shang king Diyi, King Wen of Zhou was supposed to have written at least the texts for the hexagrams and perhaps those for the lines as well. The actual hexagrams themselves were ascribed either to King Wen or to Fúxī (伏犧), a mythical prehistoric emperor who was also credited with inventing the eight trigrams and, among other things, fishing, herding, and writing.

My own hypothesis is that the text was compiled by diviners, beginning around 1000 B.C., and that it was more or less as it is now by at least 500 B.C., and probably as early as around 700 B.C. The hexagrams and the divinatory tradition probably antedate the text.

The best evidence for compilation is that the text can be analyzed into two apparent layers, which may be termed "images" and "omens." The images present images or events that illustrate the meaning of a hexagram or line. The omens comment on the auspiciousness of the hexagram or line or recommend a course of action. For example, the first line of the first hexagram QIÁN (1) STRONG ACTION: "The dragon remains underwater [image]. He must not act [omen]." Or the top line of DÀ YǑU (14) GREAT WEALTH: "Aided by Heaven [image]. Auspicious [omen]. Favorable to anything [omen]."

The omens are a kind of commentary on the images, seemingly added later. This was probably not a simple process of one person writing a commentary of omens on a preexisting text of images. Since some images cannot stand alone, they may have been written at the same time as the omens attached to them.

Those who favor the theory that the text is not a compilation but was written by one man at one time point to the consistency of the *Changes'* symbol system and of the vocabulary used throughout the text. In fact, however, the consistency in both areas is less than complete and can better be explained by the notion that the *Changes* represents the cumulative lore of a particular school of diviners.

As for the dates of the two layers of the text, the omens are quite difficult to date, since they are written in a limited technical vocabulary that could easily have been used by diviners over several centuries. However, this jargon does include a number of expressions common in Shang oracle records and early Zhou bronze inscriptions, so it probably has its origins in early Western Zhou or Shang.[4]

Some of the images can be dated to early Western Zhou by their use of words and phrases common at that time but not used later.[5] Moreover, nowhere in the *Changes* is a historical event or personage referred to that postdates the conquest by more than ten years. In one case, a Zhou prince is referred to by a title he abandoned within a few years after the conquest and which was not even recognized as a title by traditional commentators on the *Changes.* Only in modern times was it rediscovered, inscribed on bronze implements from the prince's tomb.[6]

The work of ancient literature that the images resemble most is the *Classic of Poetry* (詩經 *Shījīng*), which was compiled and edited around 500 B.C. from traditional songs and hymns. Both books appear to have drawn on the same fund of traditional Zhou folk and court literature, but the language of the two suggests that the *Changes* was probably written somewhat earlier.[7]

Yarrow divination is mentioned in Shang and Zhou oracle records and Zhou bronze inscriptions. Its first appearance in literature is in the *Classic of Documents* (書經 *Shūjīng*), in a passage probably written during the Western Zhou.[8] The earliest mention of the *Changes* itself comes in the *Analects* of Confucius (論語 *Lúnyǔ*), written at the beginning of the Warring States period.[9] Quotations from the *Changes* appear in the *Zuo Commentary* (左傳 *Zuǒzhuàn*), a Warring States history of the events of the Spring and Autumn period.

The *Zuo Commentary* records a number of divinations, giving the name of the hexagram received and often quoting a line of text. A few of these divinations are translated in Appendix B. In divinations where the *Changes* is mentioned by name, the quoted text matches up exactly with the *Changes* as we know it. In other cases, the name of a *Changes* hexagram is used, but the quotation is completely different from the text we know.

This indicates either that several widely varying versions of the *Changes* were in circulation at the time or that other yarrow divination books existed. Han Dynasty bibliographers mention divination books called *Liánshān* (連山) and *Guīcáng* (歸藏), saying that they date from the legendary Xia and the Shang Dynasty, respectively. This is possible, but it is also possible that they were both written during Warring States, perhaps on the model of the *Changes*.

It was during Warring States and Han that the *Changes* began to be regarded as more than a divination book. Commentaries were written that drew principles of conduct from its text and the hexagrams themselves became a model of the workings of the universe. The ethical commentaries reflect the influence of Confucian ethics. The metaphysical commentaries follow a direction that was apparently first taken by diviners and shamans themselves, but that later became associated with Taoism.

By the time that the *Zuo Commentary* was written, diviners had already begun to give each trigram an array of associations not directly justified by the text, such as with a natural phenomenon (wind, mountain, et al.) and with a family member (elder brother, mother, et al.). The list of associations was expanded in the commentaries, which also began to analyze the hexagrams in terms of transformations among "hard" (solid) and "soft" (broken) lines.

Several of the commentaries written during Warring States, Qin, and Han were appended to the *Changes* (易 *Yì*) to make up the *Classic of Change* or *I Ching* (易經 *Yìjīng*). Together these commentaries are known as the *Ten Wings* (十翼 *Shíyì*). Various of them elaborate the symbolism and structure of the *Changes*, use it to create a profound and suggestive metaphysics, and expound on the text's ethical meaning. The simple divinatory meaning of the *Changes* was obscured as the *Classic of Change* became a bible for many philosophical schools.

In his *Science and Civilisation in China*, Needham blames the *Classic of Change* for retarding the progress of Chinese science. He says that science became a kind of alchemy based on identification of natural elements with trigrams and on analyzing natural processes in terms of transformations among the trigrams.[10]

Right up until this century, the *Changes* continued to be viewed from perspectives suggested by the *Ten Wings*. But archaeological discoveries and a more scientific way of studying ancient history have now led many scholars to realize that the *Classic of Change* is not the original *Changes*. Chinese scholars have tried to rediscover the original *Changes* by comparing the text with other ancient writings and looking at it in the light of archaeological findings.

The text The text of the *Changes* was first written down before 500 B.C., at a time when the Chinese writing system was not as precise or as fixed as it later became. One character could be used to represent several homonyms and one word might be represented by several different characters, depending on the scribe. Add to this the fact that there was a significant reform of the writing system between 300 and 200 B.C. and we can see why the *Changes* as we know it is certainly not exactly the same as it began.

This is confirmed by the orthographic peculiarities of the earliest surviving text, which was excavated in 1976 at a place called Mǎwáng Duī (馬王堆) from a tomb of 168 B.C. It is largely the same as today's standard text and both of them are evidently versions of the same original, but there are nonetheless a number of differing readings. Most of these involve using different characters with similar pronunciations, similar meanings, or similar appearances. Another difference between the two texts lies in the arrangement of the hexagrams. The standard text puts them in a sequence based on their meanings, whereas the Mawang Dui text arranges them by their structure.[11]

The next-oldest surviving text is an incomplete one, carved in stone in 183 A.D. It is somewhat more similar to the standard text, but there remain a number of minor differences. In addition to these two texts, individual lines or phrases from the *Changes* appear in a number of other Han books.

The texts considered standard today are two Tang Dynasty versions of the *Changes*, both written around the seventh century A.D. One is the *Collected Commentaries on the Changes of Zhou* (周易集解 *Zhōuyì Jíjiě*) by Lǐ Dǐngzuò (李鼎祚). The other is the *Correct Meaning of the Changes of Zhou* (周易正義 *Zhōuyì Zhèngyì*) by Kǒng Yǐngdá (孔穎達). Both come down to us in editions printed during the Song Dynasty, about 1000 A.D.

One of the results of modern scholarship has been to propose various emendations to the standard text to bring it closer to the original. A number of these are incorporated into the text translated here.

The translation This translation differs from others in being an attempt to rediscover an original *Changes* antecedent to the commentaries. The *Changes* it translates is not a philosophical treatise but a practical manual of magical statecraft and a work of literature.

Its tone is more direct and its omens less ambiguous than those of other translations.

The translation depends on the work of modern Chinese commentators such as Li Han-san and Gao Heng whose bias is historical and philological rather than traditional and symbolistic, but also draws on my own understanding of the *Changes'* symbolism to solve some of the ambiguities in the text. This biases the translation, but seemed preferable to the practice of simply following traditional interpretations, a number of which have been demonstrated to be incorrect. The *Changes* is one of the most difficult works of Chinese literature and no translation can be guaranteed entirely accurate.

For each hexagram, I have translated the text that describes the hexagram as a whole and the texts attached to each of its lines and have given a commentary on each to elucidate its meaning and suggest how it fits into the *Changes'* symbol system. Additional points are dealt with in the notes that follow each hexagram. There is a section to explain the structure of each hexagram and one to explain how it fits into the sequence of hexagrams.

Some users of previous translations have complained that references to wars, sacrifices, noblemen, and other features of ancient society reduce the book's relevance to their own lives. They will find the present translation even less to their liking. The *Changes'* symbol system is so powerful and versatile that any number of versions of the *Changes* could be written, but as long as we translate the one that was written we must understand it on its own terms. This does not preclude relevance to our own lives. It requires only a little imagination to see how similar — sometimes unfortunately so — our behavior is to that of the ancients.

Notes

1. *Classic of Documents* (*Shūjīng* 書經), "The Oath at Muye" section (*Mùshì* 牧誓).

2. Gernet (1968), page 62.

3. Yan (1969) and Qu (1950) date it to the time of the conquest. Taguchi (1960) says early Western Zhou. Li (1947) makes it late Western Zhou. Guo (1940) and Xu(1962) both date it Warring States and Honda (1960) says it was compiled over the years from Shang to Warring States. Taguchi and Li agree that it was compiled. Qu, Xu, and Guo all say it was written by one man, but they differ by several centuries as to by whom.

4. See Yan (1969), page 16ff.

5. See Qu (1950) and Li (1969), page 140.

6. See Gu (1931), page 17ff.

7. Shchutskii (1979) thought the *Poetry* earlier. Traditionally the *Changes* was thought earlier. See also Li (1979), page 141ff.

8. See Chang Cheng-lang (1980) and Zhang Yachu (1982), and Appendix B, page 217–18.

9. The *Analects* includes one direct mention of the *Changes* and one quote from it. Both of these are doubted by some scholars. See Guo (1940), page 17ff, against and Gao (1958), page 7f, for.

10. Needham (1956), page 336.

11. See Loewe (1977) and *Wénwù* 文物 1974, numbers 7 and 9, 1978, number 8, and 1984, number 3 (Peking).

THE
SIXTY-FOUR
HEXAGRAMS

1

≡≡≡ 乾

QIÁN

STRONG ACTION

Strong action.
Strong action will be supremely blessed.
It is favorable to keep on.

Because it is made up entirely of solid, active lines, this hexagram represents pure strength and energy. The person it applies to is strong and should act. His symbol is a dragon, a creature the Chinese regarded as dangerously powerful but auspicious. In later times, the dragon became a symbol of the emperor. Here, however, it represents someone who is strong but only beginning his rise toward high rank.[1]

Lines

first line/9 —— The dragon remains underwater.
He must not act.

The dragon that remains underwater is someone strong whose time for action has not yet come. Dragons were believed to live underwater as the rulers of rivers and lakes. By leaping up into the sky, they brought rain for the crops. Although Chinese and Western dragons are similar in being powerful supernatural creatures, the moist benevolence of Chinese dragons is very much unlike Western dragons' fiery subterranean malevolence. This first line is at the bottom of the hexagram and therefore early in the development of the situation that the hexagram as a whole portrays.[2]

line two/9 —— The dragon appears in the fields.
He should go to see someone big.

As soon as he emerges from his underwater home into the world of men, the dragon should immediately seek the help of someone greater than himself. Line two is the place of the subject, who needs his ruler's help.[3, 4]

line three/9 ——— All day the lord is active,
　　　　　　　　At night he remains alert.
　　　　　　　　There is danger,
　　　　　　　　　　but he comes to no harm.

Constant energy and alertness protect him from harm. The "lord" and the "dragon" are the same person. Line three is the place of danger.[5]

line four/9 ——— If he leaps, he will land in a pool
　　　　　　　　And come to no harm.

If the dragon strives upward, he will find a comfortable place to land. This deep pool is a place of safety. It probably symbolizes a position at the ruler's court. Line four is the place of the high officer.

line five/9 ——— The dragon flies in the sky.
　　　　　　　　He should go to see someone big.

He cannot succeed on his own in these exalted regions and must find someone who can guide him. Line five is the place of the ruler, whom he seeks.[3]

top line/9 ——— The dragon reaches his limit.
　　　　　　　　Regret.

He would have been able to go farther if he had found someone to guide him. See line five. The top line of a hexagram often has to do with going too far.

all lines 9 ——— A band of dragons appears,
　　　　　　　　Among whom none is chief.
　　　　　　　　Auspicious.

He is one of a team of powerful equals. The "dragons" are the hexagram's six strong and active solid lines. Each of them is strong; together they are almost invincible. This is the only place in the *Changes* where equality is considered a good thing. Compare with BǏ (8) ALLIANCE, top line: "An alliance with no head. Inauspicious."

STRUCTURE ☰ 乾 Qián   Strong Action
          ☰ 乾 Qián   Strong Action

This hexagram is made up entirely of solid lines — symbols of strength, solidity, and action. The next hexagram KŪN (2) AC-QUIESCENCE is made up entirely of broken lines, which symbolize the opposite but complementary qualities of weakness, acquiescence, and passivity.

SEQUENCE   The *Changes* begins when its protagonist takes action. The second hexagram ACQUIESCENCE shows him becoming passive in order to consolidate his foothold in the world he has entered. His entire career, which approximates the rise to power of the Zhou (see Introduction), can be followed through the sequence of the hexagrams. This first hexagram, despite its strength, is only the beginning of that rise.

Notes

1. QIÁN — All the pronunciations in this book are given in modern standard Mandarin Chinese. The character 乾, which is used to write the name of the hexagram, contains the element 乾 "sun" and has the primary meaning "sun-dried." This gives it connotations of hardness, brightness, and fiery heat.

2. "first line/9" — The 9 here and the 6 found in other hexagrams both have to do with divination practices. See Introduction, pages 7–8.

3. "someone big" (lines two and five) — Most traditional commentators see the dragon as the "someone big."

4. "the place of the subject" (commentary on line two) — Each of the six possible places in a hexagram has its own characteristic range of meaning. Line two usually has to do with a subject or subordinate, line three with danger or misfortune, line five with the ruler, etc. For a complete outline, see Introduction, page 5.

5. "lord" (line three) — This is "lord" in the sense of "nobleman" rather than "ruler." The word 君子 *jūnzǐ* "lord" is often translated "superior man," but this is a meaning it was given later by Confucian commentators.

2

=== ≪ KŪN

ACQUIESCENCE

> Acquiescence.
> Acquiescence will be supremely blessed.
> Continue docile as a mare.
> If the lord makes a journey,
>   first he will lose his way,
>   then he will find a ruler.
> Retreating gains friends,
>   advancing loses friends.
> Staying at rest brings good fortune.

Inactivity, retreat, and obedience are three aspects of the meaning of this hexagram. Despite its negativity, it is among the greatest and most auspicious of all the hexagrams, "supremely blessed." Its subject need not be thought of as absolutely weak, since he is referred to as a "lord."[1, 2]

Lines

first line/6 — —   He treads on frost.
                     Solid ice is coming.

Winter approaches. Movement turns to immobility. QIÁN (1) STRONG ACTION turns to KŪN (2) ACQUIESCENCE. This lowest line is often associated with feet.

line two/6 — —   He is dutiful and correct.
                    Though this does not support great deeds,
                        it is still favorable.

It is better to be a faithful follower than to attempt great deeds on one's own. Line two is the place of the subject, who dutifully obeys his ruler.[3, 4]

line three/6 —— Though his brilliance is hidden,
        he may stay as he is.
    In the service of the king,
        though at first he gets nothing,
        in the end he will have success.

As the servant of a great ruler, at first he is given no chance to display his talents. In the end, however, he will demonstrate his ability and rise to high position, higher than he could have achieved on his own. Line three is the place of danger. The danger in passive acquiescence is that one may not get an opportunity to advance.[5]

line four/6 —— A closed quiver.
    No harm — no praise.

His talents remain unused, like arrows in a closed quiver. He avoids any chance of harm, but also misses any chance of winning praise and advancement. Line four is the place of the officer, who here remains inactive, either by choice or because his ruler makes no use of him.[6]

line five/6 —— Yellow skirt.
    Supremely auspicious.

Like a bright yellow skirt, he is brilliant but in a comparatively low position. Line five is the place of the ruler. The skirt symbolizes a king's chief minister. This is the height of the good fortune that can be achieved by acquiescence. The ruler is like the sun and bathes his minister in the yellow sunlight of his favor. The color yellow is associated with loyalty.[7]

top line/6 —— Streaming with blood,
    Dragons battle in the wilds.

Two great powers do battle. Neither one will escape harm. In this top line, acquiescence crosses over into activity again. A passive power becomes active. The top line of a hexagram has to do with conflict between subordinate and superior.[8]

all lines 6 —— It is favorable to remain just as one is.

STRUCTURE ☷ ⦗⦗ Kūn   Acquiescent
           ☷ ⦗⦗ Kūn   Acquiescent

This hexagram is composed entirely of broken lines, which symbolize weakness, passivity, acceptance, obedience, and withdrawal.

SEQUENCE   The active protagonist who entered the world in QIÁN (1) STRONG ACTION must attach himself acquiescently to a greater power if he is to get very far. These first two hexagrams are the positive and negative poles around which the field of the *Changes* is generated. STRONG ACTION is composed of solid, active lines and ACQUIESCENCE of broken, passive lines. All the rest of the hexagrams contain both kinds of lines and their meanings combine action and acquiescence.

Notes

1. KŪN — This hexagram is like water, which acquiescently follows the lay of the land. During the Han Dynasty (circa 200 B.C.–200 A.D.), the name of the hexagram was sometimes written with the character ⦗⦗ or ⦗⦗, which means "flowing water." The character 坤 has been standard since at least the Han period. It contains the element 土 "earth" and the hexagram has therefore traditionally been associated with earth rather than water. I prefer ⦗⦗ because line one refers indirectly to water, because forms of this character are used in the earliest surviving manuscripts, and because the figure ⩘ ("666" in ancient script) is the most ancient way of drawing the trigram ☷.

2. "retreating," "advancing" (opening text) — These are literally "southwest" and "northeast," respectively. The Zhou had their home far to the southwest of the Shang capital of China. For them, to go northeast was to advance and to go southwest was to retreat.

3. "dutiful and correct" (line two) — These are literally "straight" 直 *zhí* and "square" 方 *fāng*. The words are probably derived from either tailoring or carpentry.

4. "does not support great deeds" (line two) — The basic meaning of the word 習 *xí* "support" is "repeat." It was used in divination to refer to a second divination that supported the verdict of the first. The use of the word here is an indication that the ancient diviners who created the *Changes* may have divined each question more than once. Some sources suggest that three separate *Changes* divinations were made on each question, others that the *Changes* was used to confirm an earlier oracle bone divination (see Introduction, pages 7–8).

5. "brilliance" (line three) — The basic meaning of the word 章 *zhāng* is "bright pattern." It is used to refer to talent or ability.

6. "quiver" (line four) — The type of quiver referred to is one made of cloth and was closed with a drawstring.

7. "Yellow skirt." (line five) — Hsu (1984) suggests that *huáng* "yellow" 黃 should be read as 璜 *huáng* "jade pendant." The line would then translate: "A skirt with jade pendants." Members of the ruling classes often used to wear sets of jade pendants dangling on a cord from the sash at their waists. The *huáng* was a semicircular jade that was often the main piece of the set.

8. "streaming with blood" (top line) — The transmitted text has 玄黃 *xuān huáng* "black and yellow." Traditional interpreters say this means that one dragon bleeds black and the other yellow. I follow Gao (1947) in reading the two characters as 泫潢 *xuànhuáng* "streaming," "sweating profusely."

3

䷂ 屯

TÚN

GATHERING
SUPPORT

Gathering support.
Gathering support is supremely blessed.
It is favorable to continue.
Do not advance.
It is favorable to appoint officers.

Before setting out to do something, one must first pause to gather support or resources. This initial delay will make possible eventual great success.[1]

Lines

first line/9 —— Hesitating.
It is favorable to stay where one is.
It is favorable to appoint officers.

He hesitates because he is not yet strong enough to advance safely. He should get help before he sets out. This lowest line represents someone small or in a low position.[1]

line two/6 —— —— Gathered together but halted,
His horses and chariots stand arrayed.
Not plunder but marriage.
The lady refuses to wed,
She will wed in ten years.

He has gathered enough support to advance, but the person whom he goes to join will not accept him. All he can do is wait. Line two is the place of the subject, who seeks to join his ruler. The "lady" represents the ruler. The ruler/lady accepts or rejects the subject/suitor.[2]

line three/6 — —   He hunts without a huntsman.
                   When the deer enter the forest,
                      the lord should not follow
                      but let them go.
                   Advancing leads to trouble.

If he goes ahead without the proper help, he will get into difficulties. Line three is almost always inauspicious.

line four/6 — —   His horses and chariots stand arrayed.
                  He seeks marriage.
                  It is auspicious for him to go forward,
                     no longer unfavorable.

Not only has he gathered enough support that he is strong enough to go forward, but the person whom he goes to join is ready to accept him. Line four is the place of the officer, the king's assistant. It often involves movement after a delay and presents the solution to a problem encountered previously — in this case, in line two.[2]

line five/9 ———   Hoarding fat meat.
                  For someone small, this is auspicious.
                  For someone big, it is not.

Someone who has few resources should continue to accumulate more. But someone who already has great resources should start to make use of them. Line five is the place of the ruler, who should spend his resources for his subjects' benefit and not just hoard them for himself.[3]

top line /6 — —   His horses and chariots stand arrayed.
                  Tears and blood flow.

He did not advance and make use of his resources when he could have and now it is too late. His strength seems a threat to someone even stronger, who attacks him. "Marriage" is no longer possible. Because this top line is above the line of the ruler (line five), it often represents someone who sets himself above his ruler and describes the conflict that ensues.[2]

STRUCTURE   ☵ 坎 Kǎn   Pit (difficulties)
            ☳ 震 Zhèn   Thunderbolt (rush forward)

If he rushes forward (lower trigram ☳), he will get into difficulties (upper trigram ☵). The active first line (——) gathers up the passive lines two through four (☷) against the solid line five, which makes active use of them (——).

SEQUENCE   The first two hexagrams represented the basic active and passive principles on which the *Changes* is built. In GATHERING SUPPORT, the two principles mix together for the first time. The protagonist delays (passive) taking action (active) until he has gathered support and the action he takes then is to subordinate himself (passively) to someone greater. The hexagram can be thought of as a kind of pregnancy, a period of secluded growth before the young creature fully enters the world. The next hexagram MÉNG (4) THE YOUNG SHOOT represents childhood.

Notes

1. "appoint officers" (opening text and first line) — The words 建 侯 *jiàn hóu* literally mean "establish marquises." This refers to the Zhou kings' practice of enfieffing their more powerful followers with noble rank, land, and people in return for support.

2. "horses and chariots" (lines two, four, and top line) — At the time of the *Changes*, the Chinese did not ride horses but only used them — in pairs and fours — to pull chariots and carriages. They did not begin riding them until later in the Zhou period, when faced with the threat of mounted nomad raiders.

3. "fat meat" (line five) — Meat was a delicacy reserved almost exclusively for the nobility. Fat meat was apparently considered the best. See DǏNG (50) THE RITUAL CALDRON, line three.

4

 蒙 MÉNG

THE YOUNG SHOOT

The young shoot.
The young shoot is blessed.
"It is not I who seek something of the young shoot,
It is the young shoot who seeks something of me.
But when I have given him the first answer,
He ignores the second and the third.
Since he ignores them, I will not give them."
It is favorable to remain as one is.

If an inexperienced youth (a "young shoot") does not accept instruction and restraint, his ignorance of the world will lead him into trouble. Rather than charging ahead recklessly, he should stay as he is. The passage in quotes is probably provided for the diviner to repeat as his own words, but may also be seen as spoken by the power behind the *Changes*. As translated, it suggests that ancient diviners made each divination three times, using the second and third answers to verify the first.[1, 2]

Lines

first line/6 — —   The young shoot bursts forth.
                   Punishment should be imposed.
                   Letting him advance unshackled
                     will lead to trouble.

The exuberant youth is blind to the dangers that lie ahead of him.[3]

line two/9 ——   He wraps an offering of young shoots.
      Auspicious.
      It is auspicious for him to get a wife.
      A son can have his own household.

People who were not wealthy enough to have special bronze sacrificial vessels wrapped their offerings to the spirits in the leaves of certain plants. His offering of young shoots is a paltry one, but it indicates at least that he is ready to take a place in the world. Since line two is the place of the subject, the "wife" may symbolize his ruler.[4]

line three/6 — —   He must not take a wife.
      The gold that he sees is not for him.
      Unfavorable.

It is not favorable for him to marry. The person whom he wants to join is either too good for him or not as good as she/he seems. Line three is almost always dangerous.[5]

line four/6 — —   The young shoot is overburdened.
      Trouble.

He takes on responsibilities that are too heavy for him. Line four is the place of the officer.

line five/6 — —   The young shoot.
      Has good fortune.

He has good fortune because he accepts restraint. The upper trigram Gèn ☶ Keep Still indicates restraint. Line five is the place of the ruler. The passive line (— —) shows the subject's acceptance of his ruler's restraint. Line five is also usually the place of greatest good fortune in a hexagram.

top line/9 ——   The young shoot is caught and bound.
      It is not favorable to make raids,
      It is favorable to ward them off.

He recklessly goes too far and is restrained by force. The top line of a hexagram often has to do with going too far and with conflict between inferior and superior. The solid line suggests both the inferior's reckless activity and the superior's solid restraint.

STRUCTURE ☶ 艮 Gēn   Keep Still (stopped, restraint)
            ☵ 坎 Kǎn   Pit (danger, difficulties, trouble)

Trouble is stopped. Someone smaller or lower is in difficulties (lower trigram ☵). Someone bigger or higher restrains him (upper trigram ☶).

SEQUENCE   If TÚN (3) GATHERING SUPPORT was pregnancy, this hexagram is childhood, when the young creature is subject to his parents' restraint and instruction. The restraint in GATHERING SUPPORT was self-restraint. The restraint in THE YOUNG SHOOT is imposed from outside.

Notes

1. MÉNG — the word 蒙 *méng* can have several meanings: "young shoot," "darkness," "blindness," "ignorance," "to cover," "to receive." Which of these were in the minds of the early diviners, I am not sure. The young shoot is in darkness, covered by soil and ignorant of the world outside.

2. "But when I have given him the first answer, he ignores the second and the third. Since he ignores them, I will not give them." (opening text) — This passage is usually interpreted: "But when I have answered his question once, he insults me by asking it a second and a third time. Since he insults me, I will not answer." Both interpretations are reasonable. For more evidence that ancient diviners may have asked each question more than once, see KŪN (2) ACQUIESCENCE, note 4, and BǏ (8) ALLIANCE, note 2. See also Gao (1947), pages 8–9.

3. "unshackled" (first line) — The words 桎梏 *zhì gù* refer to wooden fetters for the feet and the hands, respectively.

4. "wraps an offering" (line two) — See also TÀI (11) FLOWING, line two, and PǏ (12) BLOCKED, lines two and three.

5. "gold" (line three) — At the time of the *Changes*, the word 金 *jīn* "metal" probably referred to bronze rather than to gold. Only later, when gold became the metal par excellence, did it come to mean gold. I have nonetheless chosen to translate it "gold" because during the Bronze Age bronze had the symbolic value that gold has for us today. In fact, not only was it the most brilliant metal but the hardest as well. Wealthy lords held much of their portable wealth in objects made of bronze.

5

䷄ 濡 RÚ

GETTING WET

Getting wet.
Shining allegiance will be blessed.
Keeping on will bring good fortune.
It is favorable to ford a great river.

He boldly sets out to ford a broad and dangerous river. Although he gets wet, he succeeds in reaching the far shore. Bold action and clear allegiance to a superior are what ensure success. In the *Changes*, fording a river symbolizes any difficult task or ordeal.[1, 2]

Lines

first line/9 ——
He gets wet in the fields.
He should stay there. No harm.

Difficulties at the beginning of a journey are a warning of worse to come. The way to escape harm is to stay where one is.

line two/9 ——
He gets wet on the sand.
Words are spoken against him,
But he is fortunate in the end.

Getting a bit wet on the shore of the river is no disaster. It will not prevent his getting across. Line two is the place of the subject, who goes to enter his ruler's service. Loose sand is like slander. Though members of the ruler's entourage speak against him, he is accepted in the end.

line three/9 ——
Getting wet in the mud
Causes raiders to come.

He advances too far and becomes stuck in the mud of the river bottom. Being dirty makes him look like a dirty rebel. Being stuck makes him vulnerable to attack. This uppermost line of the lower trigram often portrays the misfortunes of someone who tries to advance beyond his proper station.[3]

line four/6 — —   Soaked with blood,
                   He emerges from his hole.

He does not leave home until he is forced to. He should have gone sooner. Line four, coming just after the midpoint of the hexagram, sometimes refers to being late. See GUĪ MÈI (54) A MAIDEN MARRIES. This line and the top line refer to holes because, as the two broken lines of the trigram Kǎn ☵ Pit, they symbolize two pits.[4]

line five/9 ———   Soaked with food and wine.
                   Perseverance brings good fortune.

He celebrates a successful crossing, being welcomed by the ruler whom he crossed the river to join. Line five is the place of the ruler and of success. The active line (———) suggests that success is achieved by taking action.

top line/6 — —   Into his hole
                   Come three uninvited guests.
                   If he honors them, all will be well.

He delays leaving home for so long that someone comes to get him, someone who can either help or destroy him. The "three guests" are symbolized by the three solid lines of the lower trigram Qián ☰ Strong Action.[4]

STRUCTURE ☵ 坎 Kǎn   Pit (difficulties)
          ☰ 乾 Qián   Strong Action
Strong action (lower trigram ☰) will overcome the difficulties that lie ahead (upper trigram ☵).

SEQUENCE   This is the hexagram in which the protagonist leaves home to go and take a place in the outside world. In TŪN (3) GATHERING SUPPORT, he restrained himself until he had gathered enough support to be able to advance safely. In MĚNG (4) THE YOUNG SHOOT, he was restrained by someone else from a reckless advance. In GETTING WET, he braves difficulties to go and enter the entourage of his ruler.

Notes

1. GETTING WET — The traditional text has 需 xū "wait" rather than 濡 rú "get wet." In ancient times, both words were written in the same way (as 需). I base my reading on context, on the hexagram's structure, and on the fact that of the two words only 濡 "get wet" occurs elsewhere in the *Changes*, which it does several times (in hexagrams 22, 43, 63, and 64).

2. "allegiance" (opening text) — The word 孚 fú means "allegiance," "faithfulness," "faith," "trust." This was one of the most important virtues at the time of the *Changes* and a basis of the social order.

3. "raiders" (line three) — The word 寇 kòu "raid," "raiders," is the same word used in the Shang oracle records in referring to raids against Zhou.

4. "hole" (line four, top line) — In some areas of western China near the ancient Zhou homeland, people still live in cave houses neatly dug into the side of a hill and fitted with doors and windows. This may be why the word 穴 xué "hole" is used to refer to a home. In other parts of ancient north China, people lived in sunken-floored huts that might also have been referred to as "holes."

6

☰☵ 訟   SÒNG

GRIEVANCE

Grievance.
Allegiance is blocked and becomes cautious.
To stop halfway is auspicious,
To carry on to the end is not.
One should go to see a big man.
One should not cross a big river.

Because he has not been granted advancement, a subject's faith in
his ruler is impaired and he feels a grievance. Rather than let this
continue, he should go and have the matter out ("go to see a big
man"). He should not attempt any great undertaking ("cross a big
river").[1]

Lines

first line/6 — —   He quits his ruler's service.
                     Words are spoken against him,
                     But he is fortunate in the end.

It is better for him to quit now than to wait until a bad situation
becomes worse. This line is early enough in the hexagram that he
can still back out safely, suffering nothing worse than a little criticism. The passive line (— —) suggests withdrawal.

line two/9 ——   His grievance is rejected.
                     He flees to his 300-household estate
                     And escapes disaster.

When his grievance is rejected, he withdraws from his ruler's service and retires to his own estate. Commentators say that a 300-household estate was a small one. This solid second line of the trigram Kǎn ☵ Pit (danger) stands for safety in the midst of danger.[2]

line three/6 — — He lives off his patrimony.
                    This is dangerous,
                        but will be fortunate in the end.
                    In the service of the king,
                        he would achieve nothing.

His inherited estate is just barely enough to live on. It is better for him to stay on it, however, than to enter the service of the king.

line four/9 —— His grievance is rejected.
                    He returns to obedience.
                    Though he suffers loss,
                        it is auspicious for him to stay as he is.

When his ruler rejects his grievance, he abandons it and once again becomes a docile subject. Line four is the place of the officer, whose obedience will be rewarded with advancement. Compare with line two.

line five/9 —— He makes a grievance.
                    Supremely auspicious.

His grievance is accepted and he is granted advancement. Line five is the place of success and of the ruler, to whom the grievance is made.

top line/9 —— He is awarded a leather belt,
                    But in a morning,
                        it is taken from him three times.

The leather belt is a mark of honor given to him by the king. The grievance by which he gained it, however, created an atmosphere of mistrust that leads to its being taken away again. The top line of a hexagram often involves conflict with a superior. The number three is related to the three strong lines of the upper trigram Qián ☰ Strong Action. For something similar, see the top line of the previous hexagram RÚ (5) GETTING WET.

STRUCTURE ☰ 乾 Qián   Strong Action
          ☵ 坎 Kǎn   Pit (difficulties)

The subject is in difficulties (lower trigram ☵), his path ahead blocked by the strong ruler (upper trigram ☰). He therefore lays his difficulties (lower trigram) before his ruler (upper trigram) in a grievance.

SEQUENCE   His ruler, whose service he braved difficulties to join in RÚ (5) GETTING WET, does not grant him the advancement he seeks, so he makes a grievance.

Notes

1. SÒNG — The word 訟 *sòng* "grievance" refers to legal proceedings. It is made up of elements that mean "speak" 言 and "duke" 公. "Speaking to the duke" is taking a case to court. The English word "court" itself refers to a nobleman's courtyard, the place where his subjects brought their disputes and grievances for him to hear.

2. line two — The usual interpretation of this line — and also a reasonable one — is that the fugitive flees even his own estate, thereby saving its 300 households from the disaster of attack by the offended ruler.

7

☷☵ 師 SHĪ

AN ARMY

An army.
For a big man,
    keeping on will bring good fortune
    and no harm.

Being in an army is dangerous, but the army gives its "big men" (strong warriors) opportunities for advancement and gain. The key military virtues, according to the text, are discipline and caution. Followers should follow and leaders should lead and the army as a whole should not advance too quickly or too far.

Lines

first line/6 — —   An army sets out in strict order.
                 If not, even the strongest is doomed.

Order and discipline are essential to an army's success. This lowest line represents a soldier of the lowest rank. As the first line, it has to do with setting out. "Strongest" may refer either to an army or to a man.

line two/9 ——   In an army.
               Good fortune. No harm.
               The king thrice awards him rank.

The king picks a strong warrior out from among the other soldiers and gives him a position of leadership. Line two is the place of the subject. The strong line represents a strong warrior.[1]

line three/6 — —   An army carts corpses.
                  Misfortune.

Defeat. The army should avoid battle. Line three is almost always inauspicious.

line four/6 — —   An army encamps away from the enemy.
                   And avoids harm.

The army saves itself by avoiding battle. Line four is often the solution to a problem encountered in line three. The passive line (— —) suggests that the solution in this case involves inaction or retreat.[2]

line five/6 — —   The hunt has reaped its harvest.
                   Interrogating prisoners will avert harm.
                   Let the elder son lead the army.
                   If the younger son did,
                        there would be cartloads of dead.
                   Persevering brings misfortune.

Be satisfied with the gains you have made; go no further. By interrogating prisoners, you can learn about the enemy and will be able to decide how best to act. The "elder son" is the stronger and more experienced of two people. It is the "younger son" to whom this line is addressed. The line is passive and in the place of the ruler. This suggests both that the ruler should be passive and that the subject should be passive toward his ruler.

top line/6 — —   The great lords receive mandates
                   To found states and establish their houses.

The king rewards his commanders with land and noble titles that they can pass on to their descendants.

STRUCTURE ☷ 〣 Kūn   Acquiescent (passive, obedient,
                                accepting, a crowd)
           ☵ 坎 Kǎn   Pit (danger, difficulties)

The members of an army face danger (lower trigram ☵) with passive obedience (upper trigram ☷). The army's commander responds to danger (☵) by remaining passive (☷). The broken lines are a crowd of soldiers. The solid line is a strong warrior among them. He is accepted forward into high position by the commander (upper trigram ☷).

SEQUENCE   The subject's request for advancement was rejected in the previous hexagram SONG (6) GRIEVANCE. Now he serves loyally as a common soldier, facing danger on his ruler's behalf. He will be rewarded with the advancement he sought.

Notes

1. "thrice" (line two) — This may simply serve to emphasize the value of the award. See also RÚ (5) GETTING WET, top line, SÒNG (6) GRIEVANCE, top line, and BǏ (8) ALLIANCE, line five. The numbers three, seven, and ten occur frequently in the *Changes*. Their significance is not always clear.

2. "encamps away from the enemy" (line four) — This is literally "encamps on the left." Commentators say that the left is the direction of retreat.

8

≡≡ 比

BǏ

ALLIANCE

Alliance brings good fortune.
Even though the original divination said:
   "Keep right on as you are. No harm."
After unrest begins, this is inauspicious.

Allying oneself with someone stronger protects one from harm.
Even though under normal circumstances one may be able to remain independent, when danger threatens one must have a
protector.[1, 2]

Lines

first line/6 — —   Faithful alliance:
                    Averts harm.
              His faithfulness overflows:
                    Unexpected trouble will end well.

Having a strong ally right from the start is a protection against harm.
One keeps an ally by being faithful to him.[3]

line two/6 — —   Alliance from within.
              Auspicious.

One gets closer to a ruler with whom one is already associated. Line
two is inside the inner trigram, therefore "within." It is the place of
the subject and is particularly auspicious here because the hexagram
as a whole recommends acting like a subject.

line three/6 — —   Alliance with the wrong man.

Line three is the place of danger. The only danger in entering into an alliance is that one might choose the wrong ally.[4]

line four/6 — —   External alliance.
                          Auspicious.

One joins someone outside. Line four is the entry into the outer trigram. It is also the place of the officer.

line five/9 ———   Shining ally.
                          The king makes a three-side hunt:
                          Though his people lose the game before them,
                          They are not blamed.
                          Auspicious.

Despite their shortcomings, the king remains a shining ally to his people. Line five is the place of the ruler. On a "three-side hunt," beaters drove game inward from three sides of a large square. The king waited on the open fourth side to shoot the game as it rushed out. In this case, his beaters let the animals in the square break out through their lines. But because these people are his faithful followers, the king does not punish them.[5]

top line/6 — —   An alliance with no head.
                          Inauspicious.

An alliance must have a head. A subject must not try to equal his ruler. This top line is above the line of the ruler, line five, and implies conflict with one's ruler.[6]

STRUCTURE ☵ 坎 Kǎn   Pit (danger)
                        ☷ 巛 Kūn   Acquiescent (obedient, a crowd)
With danger ahead (upper trigram ☵), one acquiesces (lower trigram ☷) in another's leadership. The broken lines are a crowd of passive followers who ally themselves with a strong leader, the solid line (———) in the place of the ruler, line five.

SEQUENCE   The subject of SHĪ (7) AN ARMY faced danger in his ruler's army in order to get closer to him. The protagonist of this inverse hexagram ALLIANCE gets closer to his ruler in order to be protected from harm.

Notes

1. BĬ — The word 比 *bǐ* means "side-by-side," "get close to," and "assist," as well as "enter into an alliance with."

2. "original divination" (opening text) — This is one more indication that at least some ancient diviners may have made each divination more than once. See MÉNG (4) THE YOUNG SHOOT, opening text and commentary and note 2.

3. "overflows" (first line) — This is literally "overflows the jar," referring to one of the large pottery jars in which both wine and grain were stored.

4. "wrong man" (line three) — This is literally "not-man" (非人 *fěirén*) and may also mean "bad man," which is to say "not a man," "inhuman."

5. line five — The Chinese text is ambiguous. It may also mean that the king misses game that runs out right in front of him, but his loyal people do not blame him or become apprehensive over his ability to protect them.

6. "with no head" (top line) — See also QIÁN (1) STRONG ACTION, all lines 9.

9

䷈ 小·畜 　　XIĂO XÙ

SMALL IS TAMED

Small is tamed.
Blessed.
Dense clouds but no rain
　　from our western lands.

Someone small is dangerously active but lets himself be tamed
before he goes too far. He is like a storm cloud that rises in the west
but evaporates before it turns to rain. Rain is a symbol of conflict.
The west was the homeland of the Zhou people, upon whose story
the *Changes* is based. They are being told that they are not yet strong
enough to go east and fight their Shang rulers.[1, 2]

Lines

first line/9 ——　He goes back on the road.
　　　　　　　　What harm could befall him?
　　　　　　　　Auspicious.

He wisely turns back before getting into difficulties. By taking the
same road back that he came out on, he is assured of safety.

line two/9 ——　Dragged back.
　　　　　　　　Auspicious.

As long as he turns back, it makes no difference whether he does so
voluntarily or under duress. Line two is the place of the subject, who
is under his ruler's power.

line three/9 ——　Carriage and axle part.
　　　　　　　　　Husband and wife glare at each other.

Going too far too fast causes the breakup of a relationship. Line three often shows a subject who goes too far, offending against the ruler.[3, 4]

line four/6 — —   Faithful allegiance
                  Sends sorrow far away
                  And averts harm.

In order to avoid conflict, he halts and surrenders, becoming an obedient vassal. Line four often gives the solution to a problem encountered in line three. This particular fourth line is passive (— —) and at the bottom of the trigram Xùn ☴ Kneel in Submission. Passivity and submission prevent discord.

line five/9 ———   Good fortune comes to him from his neighbor,
                  To whom he is faithful as if bound.

Line five is the place of the ruler. His "neighbor" is his ruler.

top line/9 ———   It rains. The rain ends.
                  Now he can drive forward again.
                  It is dangerous to stay passive as a wife.
                  The moon comes full.
                  But marching forth like a lord to war would bring
                     misfortune.

He went too far, causing conflict between himself and his ruler. Now that the conflict is over, it is time for him to start his carriage forward again, as long as he avoids acting aggressively. The moon's coming full may symbolize both the coming of a time for action and the subject's rise to eminence. The top line of a hexagram almost always has to do with going too far. It often involves conflict and sometimes describes a movement beyond the situation portrayed in the rest of the hexagram.[5]

STRUCTURE   ☴ 巽 Xùn   Kneel in Submission
                       ☰ 乾 Qián   Strong Action
Someone small or in a low position is very active (lower trigram ☰), but when he comes up against someone in a high position he kneels in submission (upper trigram ☴).

SEQUENCE   The events of this hexagram take place within the alliance formed in the previous hexagram BǏ (8) ALLIANCE. The lesser partner unwisely tries to push ahead too quickly but restrains himself in time to avert a clash with his ally.

Notes

1. SMALL IS TAMED — See DÀ XÙ (26) BIG IS TAMED.

2. "Dense clouds . . . western land." (opening text) — See also XIǍO GUÒ (62) SMALL GETS BY, line five.

3. "axle" (line three) — The word 輹 *fú*, translated "axle," actually refers to the wooden fitting that held the axle to the carriage. Driving ahead too fast causes it to break loose. See also DÀ XÙ (26) BIG IS TAMED, line two.

4. "Husband and wife" (line three) — The husband appears to symbolize the ruler and the wife the subject. This is opposite to TÚN (3) GATHERING SUPPORT, line two, and MÉNG (4) THE YOUNG SHOOT, as well as DÀ GUÒ (28) BIG GETS BY, line five, and GÒU (44) SUBJUGATED. In all these cases, the woman represents the ruler. The difference seems to be that when the man is a suitor and the woman his potential bride, she is the ruler; when they are already married, he is the ruler.

5. "The moon comes full." (top line) — See also GUĪ MÈI (54) A MAIDEN MARRIES, line five, and ZHŌNG FÚ (61) WHOLEHEARTED ALLEGIANCE, line four.

10

☰ 履 LǙ

TREADING

He treads on the tiger's tail,
But it does not eat him.
Blessed.

He steps forward blindly, transgressing against someone strong
enough to destroy him. The "tiger" is a powerful ruler. Fortunately,
the ruler is too powerful to feel threatened and spares him.

Lines

first line/9 ——   Plain shoes.
                   Advance unharmed.

Plain undyed cloth shoes symbolize small ambitions. They were
probably the sort of shoes worn by commoners and the minor
gentry, as opposed to the gold-embroidered shoes worn by a "shining lord" in the first line of LUÓ (30) SHINING LIGHT. The first
line of a hexagram is at its foot, so it is associated with feet.

line two/9 ——   Treading a level, easy path.
                   It is auspicious to remain in seclusion.

He does something easy and keeps out of harm's way. Line two is the
place of the subject or subordinate. Because it is within the inner
trigram, it sometimes has to do with being inside something ("in
seclusion").

line three/6 —— He sees dimly
                   And walks lame.

> He treads on the tiger's tail
> And it eats him.
> Misfortune.
> A common soldier
>   acts the great lord.

He goes a step too far, transgressing against someone powerful, who destroys him. Line three is the place of danger, where the lower trigram approaches the upper.[1]

line four/9 —— He treads on the tiger's tail.
His terror ends in good fortune.

He steps forward blindly and is terrified to discover that he has offended against his ruler. But his ruler forgives him and allows his advance, perhaps because he approves of the energy it demonstrates. Line four is the place of the officer.

line five/9 —— Torn shoes.
It is dangerous to continue.

His shoes are torn, either by his journey or by the tiger. This place of the ruler, line five, is too high for him.

top line/9 —— He watches where he treads,
he studies the signs.
He returns from his journey
with supreme good fortune.

He avoids difficulties by advancing with caution, watching where he puts his feet, and studying the omens. He is thus able to turn back at the right time.

STRUCTURE ☰ 乾 Qián   Strong Action (solid, strong)
☱ 兌 Duì   Stand Straight (break free, step forward)

Trying to stand up on his own (lower trigram ☱), he comes up against the solid obstacle of his powerful ruler (upper trigram ☰). The solid upper trigram is like a tiger's body: the broken line three (— —) is its tail and the solid lines one and two (☰) are feet treading on its tail. The hexagram's two active trigrams give it a feeling of strength and energy.

SEQUENCE   As with the previous hexagram XIĂO XÙ (9) SMALL IS TAMED, the events of this hexagram take place within the alliance formed in BǏ (8) ALLIANCE. The active subject of SMALL IS TAMED let himself be restrained before he went too far. The subject of TREADING does go too far, but his offense is pardoned. Perhaps this is in part because he does not challenge the "tiger" face-to-face but only comes up from behind and inadvertently steps on its tail.

Note

1. "He sees dimly and walks lame." (line three) — See also GUĪ MÈI (54) A MAIDEN MARRIES, first line and line two.

11

≡≡ 泰

TÀI

FLOWING

Flowing.
Small goes forward,
   big draws back.
Auspicious.
Blessed.

A smooth and easy advance. Someone small moves forward, aided by someone big, who draws back to help him. This auspicious hexagram portrays an ideal relationship between a subject and his ruler.[1, 2]

Lines

first line/9 ——   Madder is picked
                          by the roots.
                       Marching forth will bring good fortune.

One's rise starts from a low position. Madder is a low creeper, the roots of which are used to make alizarin-red dye.

line two/9 ——   He wraps the offering
                          of a poor harvest.
                       Crossing the River,
                       He will not be swept away.
                       Though his friends are lost,
                       He will gain the far shore road.

He has little, but humbly offers what he can and is helped to surmount the obstacles in his path. Line two is the place of the subject, who is aided by his ruler. The river referred to is probably the Yellow River (黄河 *Huánghé*).[3, 4]

line three/9 —— No level ground does not become hilly,
No advance does not end in retreat.
Persevere against adversity,
    you will come to no harm.
Do not fear. For the faithful
There will be food left
    when the time comes to eat.

Even though their relationship may sometimes turn sour, a subject who remains faithful to his ruler will not be abandoned. The misfortune normal to third lines is in this case somewhat mitigated, as is the auspiciousness of line four. Such a balance is usually maintained by these two lines.[5]

line four/6 — — Misfortunes
    fly to him from his neighbor,
Whom he has faith in
    and does not blame.

Line four is the place of the officer, who bears faithful allegiance to his ruler.

line five/6 — — King Diyi gave his sister in marriage
And riches besides. Supreme good fortune.

The subject receives gifts from his ruler. The second-last Shang king of China gave many gifts to his great vassal the lord of Zhou, including a bride from one of the royal clans. Line five is the place of the ruler and the passive line (— —) indicates receptivity.[6]

top line/6 — — Battlements are toppled into the ditch.
Do not field an army.
From the capital
    comes a command to halt.
Keeping on will lead to trouble.

Going too far leads to destruction. The top line of a hexagram often depicts the conflict that ensues when a subject places himself above his ruler.

STRUCTURE ☷ ☵ Kūn   Acquiescent (weak, accepting,
                                      withdraw)
             ☰ 乾 Qián   Strong Action (strong, active)

The strong and active lower trigram (☰) moves easily forward
through the weak and accepting upper trigram (☷). A strong and
active subject moves smoothly forward, aided by a ruler who accepts
the advance and draws back to help him (see opening text).

SEQUENCE   The association entered into in BĬ (8) ALLIANCE
went through some initial difficulties in XIǍO XÙ (9) SMALL IS
TAMED and LÜ (10) TREADING, but in FLOWING it reaches an
easy perfection, as subject and ruler work together for the subject's
advance.

Notes

1. TÀI — The meaning of the word 泰 tài is debatable. Its basic
meaning is "huge" or "extreme," but commentators do not use this.
Most English translators call the hexagram Peace. Chinese commentators define it with words that mean something like "getting
through," "successful," or "smooth and auspicious." I have selected
FLOWING to convey this meaning because the character 泰 contains the element 氺 , which is a form of 水 "water."

2. "Small goes forward, big draws back." (opening text) — See
next hexagram PĬ (12) BLOCKED, where these actions are reversed.

3. "He wraps the offering of a poor harvest." (line two) — This is
one of the most disputable phrases in the Changes. Various commentators and translators give it as: "Bearing with the uncultivated,"
"Encompassing the ends of the earth," "Encompassing emptiness,"
"[Floating on] a big gourd," and "Encompassing the waters."

4. "Wraps the offering" (line two) — Those too poor to own
bronze ritual vessels wrapped their offerings to the spirits in the
leaves of certain plants. See MÉNG (4) THE YOUNG SHOOT, line
two, and PĬ (12) BLOCKED, lines two and three.

5. "There will be food left" (line three) — Ancient lords held
sacrificial feasts in which they and their relatives and vassals ate the
intentional leftovers of a cooked offering to the spirits.

6. "King Diyi gave his sister in marriage" (line five) — Dìyǐ 帝
乙 was the second-last Shang king of China. The "younger sister" he
gave as a bride to the lord of Zhou was probably actually a distant
cousin. All members of a generation in the Shang clans were thought
of as brothers and sisters. In any case, this bride may have been a

very important gift. A Shang wife is said to have borne one lord of
Zhou (季歷 *Jìlì*), a son who became King Wen (文王 *Wénwáng*), the
originator of Zhou power. Another Shang wife is said to have borne
King Wen a son who became King Wu (武王 *Wǔwáng*), the conqueror of Shang and the first Zhou king of China. See also GUĪ MÈI
(54) A MAIDEN MARRIES, line five.

12

☰☷ 否   PǏ

BLOCKED

Blocked.
Do not keep on like a lord.
Big goes forward,
　　small draws back.

When one's advance is blocked by someone powerful, one must accept it and draw back. To act "like a lord" means to take strong action.[1, 2]

Lines

first line/6 — —　　Madder is picked
　　　　　　　　　by the roots.
　　　　　　　Staying as one is brings good fortune.
　　　　　　　Blessed.

It is best to remain in this low position. Madder is a low creeper, the roots of which are used to make alizarin-red dye. Though the root is low, it is the most important part of the plant.[3]

line two/6 — —　　He wraps an offering of meat.
　　　　　　　All right for a little man,
　　　　　　　But a big man is blocked.
　　　　　　　Blessed.

It is all right for someone of low status to wrap his offering in leaves, but someone greater must use bronze ritual vessels. Line two is the place of the subject or subordinate: It is he who will be blessed with an eventual successful advance.[4]

line three/6 —— He wraps an offering of sauces.

This is probably inauspicious. It is all right to offer plain meat wrapped in leaves (see line two), but meat with sauces is a fine offering that should be made in the proper bronze ritual vessels. Line three is at the top of the lower trigram. It often represents someone who strives higher than he can or should go. If he cannot afford bronze vessels, he should not offer sauced meats.[4]

line four/9 —— Awarded rank.
No harm.
An associate shines blessings.

Line four is the place of the officer. The ruler who had been blocking his advance now grants him a commission.

line five/9 —— A fortunate blockage.
Run away? Run away?
He is tied to a flourishing mulberry tree.

His advance may be blocked, but he is forced to stay in a place that is a good one. Line five is the place of the ruler. Why should he want to run away from a flourishing ruler?

top line/9 —— The blockage is overthrown.
Blocked before,
happy afterward.

The top line of a hexagram often has to do with conflict between a subject and his ruler. Usually the subject is defeated. In this case, his attack is successful.

STRUCTURE ☰ 乾 Qián   Strong Action (solid, strong, active)

☷ 巛 Kūn   Acquiescent (weak, passive, withdraw)

The weak and passive lower trigram (☷) is blocked by the strong upper trigram (☰) ahead of it. Someone small or in a low position passively accepts the fact that his progress is blocked by someone strong and in a high position. The upper trigram advances (☰), the lower trigram withdraws (☷). See opening text: "Big goes forward, small draws back."

SEQUENCE   In the previous hexagram TÀI (11) FLOWING, the ruler helped his subject to advance. Here he blocks him, not wanting him to rise too high.

Notes

1. "Blocked." (opening text) — The transmitted text has: "Blocked by someone bad." I follow Li (1969).

2. "Big goes forward, small draws back." (opening text) — Compare with the opening text of the previous hexagram TÀI (11) FLOWING: "Small goes forward, big draws back."

3. "Madder is picked by the roots." (first line) — Compare with the first line of FLOWING, which is identical, except that the omen recommends marching forth rather than staying as one is.

4. "He wraps an offering" (lines two and three) — These lines are traditionally interpreted: "He bears and endures" and "He bears shame." I follow Gao (1947) and Li (1969). See MÉNG (4) THE YOUNG SHOOT, note 4.

13

☰ 同人   TÓNG RÉN

WITH OTHERS

With others.
To be with others in the wilds is blessed.
It is favorable to ford a great river.
It is favorable to keep on like a lord.

One achieves success as an active member of an active group. "In the wilds" means out where there is an open field for action, not hemmed in. "To keep on like a lord" means to take strong action. "To ford a great river" symbolizes any difficult or dangerous ordeal or enterprise.[1]

Lines

first line/9 ——   With others at the gate.
                       He comes to no harm.

To be at the gate is safe because one is not completely enclosed. But it is not auspicious because one is not completely in the open. The first line is the hexagram's gateway and often refers to beginning something.

line two/6 — —   With others in the temple.
                       There will be trouble.

A strong group that is inactive and hemmed in will turn its destructive energies inward on its own members. The group is seen as inside something because line two is in the middle of the inner trigram. The group is inactive because the line is inactive (— —). The temple referred to is one dedicated to a clan's ancestors.

line three/9 ——   Soldiers lie hidden in the underbrush.
                  If they climb the high hill,
                  They will not rise again for three years.

They should stay hidden. This is not the time to take action. Line three is associated with danger or misfortune.[2]

line four/9 ——   Mounting the battlements,
                  They are unassailable.

It is not clear whether they mount the battlements in attack or in defense. Line four is the place in which one rises into the upper trigram.

line five/9 ——   With others, first cries and then laughter:
                  A great army conquers whom it meets.

Line five is the place of the ruler and of success.

top line/9 ——   With others in the fields.
                  No regrets.

Working on together in the open, the members of the group will achieve success. They may be fighting a war, since the top line of a hexagram is often a place of conflict.

STRUCTURE ☰ 乾 Qián   Strong Action (active, strong)
           ☲ 離 Luó   Shining Light (shining, shone upon, within)

The five strong lines represent a strong group. The one weak line (— —) is a member of it who is the subject of the hexagram. The group is strong and active in the outside world (outer trigram ☰). The individual subject is within the group and is shone upon by its or its ruler's brilliance (lower or inner trigram ☲).

SEQUENCE   Acting together with others is one way of overcoming the obstacle set up in PĬ (12) BLOCKED. Rather than advancing individually, one advances with the group.

Notes

1. "the wilds" (opening text) — The "wilds" (野 yě) are the uncultivated land beyond a town's fields. The "fields" referred to in the top line (郊 jiāo) are the cultivated land closer to the town.

2. "If they climb the high hill, they will not rise again for three years." (line three) — This can also be read: "If you climb the high hill, you will not rise again for three years."

14

䷌ 大有 DÀ YǑU

GREAT WEALTH

Great wealth.
Great wealth is supremely blessed.

Great wealth makes possible great achievement.

Lines

first line/9 —— By doing no injury,
    he averts harm.
A period of adversity
    ends without harm.

Rather than striking out against the powerful ruler who causes him adversity, the wealthy subject remains his friend.

line two/9 —— Riding a great carriage,
He advances unharmed.

His wealth and/or his association with a strong ruler allow him to go forward safely. Line two is the place of the subject or subordinate.

line three/9 —— A duke feasts the Son of Heaven.
A little man cannot.

Although the wealthy subject may be rich enough to provide a feast for the king, he does not have the high rank required by protocol and would be struck down if he dared to try. Line three, since it is at the top of the lower trigram, often shows someone in a low position overreaching himself.

line four/9 ——   By avoiding ostentation,
                    He averts harm.

Line four is the place of the officer, who must be careful not to
outshine his ruler.

line five/6 — —   Awed into allegiance.
                    Good fortune.

The wealthy subject remains faithful to his overwhelmingly powerful ruler. Line five is the place of the ruler. The passive line (— —)
indicates the subject's passive acceptance of his ruler's authority.

top line/9 ——   Aided by Heaven.
                    Auspicious.
                    Favorable to anything.

With Heaven's help, it is even possible to attack one's ruler and
succeed, as the Zhou discovered (see next hexagram QIÀN [15]
MODESTY, note 1). The top line of a hexagram is often associated
with conflict between ruler and subject. Being closest to Heaven, it
refers to Heaven more frequently than any other line.

STRUCTURE ☲ 離 Luó   Shining light (shining, shone
                       upon)
             ☰ 乾 Qián   Strong Action (active, strong)
Someone strong advances from a low position (lower trigram ☰)
either to shine or to be shone upon by someone in a high position
(upper trigram ☲).

SEQUENCE   This and the previous hexagram, its inverse
TÓNG RÉN (13) WITH OTHERS, describe ways of dealing with
the blockage set up in PǏ (12) BLOCKED. The blockage was the
result of a ruler's refusal or inability to help his subject get ahead.
The subject can overcome the blockage either by acting together
WITH OTHERS in his ruler's service or by being wealthy enough to
advance alone, beneath the ruler.

15

䷎ 謙

MODESTY

Modesty.
Modesty is blessed.
The lord will achieve success.

He is strong enough to act boldly, but modesty and caution will lead to greater success.[1]

Lines

first line/6 — —　　Modestly, modestly,
　　　　　　　　　The lord undertakes the crossing of a great river.
　　　　　　　　　Auspicious.

Modesty will bring success in a difficult undertaking. This line is doubly modest because it is both a weak line (— —) and the lowest line in the hexagram. It has to do with beginning something because it is the first line.

line two/6 — —　　His modesty is well known.
　　　　　　　　　It is auspicious for him to stay as he is.

Line two is the place of the subordinate.

line three/9 ——　　Modest despite his accomplishments,
　　　　　　　　　The lord will achieve success.
　　　　　　　　　Auspicious.

His achievements make modesty difficult, but modesty will make it possible for him to achieve even more. Line three is usually difficult or dangerous.

line four/6 — —   He modestly gives the command.
                    No longer unfavorable.

Line four is the entry into high position. It often involves movement
after a delay.[2]

line five/6 — —   Misfortunes descend on him from his neighbor.
                    It is favorable to invade,
                    No longer unfavorable.

A weak or immoral ruler is such a source of misfortune that the
strong but modest subject is forced to invade and supplant him. Line
five is the place of the ruler. Here both it (— —) and the upper
trigram (☷) are weak.

top line/6 — —   His modesty is well known.
                    It is favorable for him to field an army
                       and march against cities and states.

His modesty attracts people to his cause. They know that he would
not be taking action unless it were necessary. The top line of a
hexagram often shows a subject attacking a ruler.

STRUCTURE ☷ 〣 Kūn   Acquiescent (passive, weak)
               ☶ 艮 Gēn   Keep Still (stopped, restraint)
A subject restrains himself in a low position (lower trigram ☶),
even though his ruler is weak (upper trigram ☷). There is nothing
to prevent the subject from advancing, but he stays where he is.

SEQUENCE   The protagonist of the last two hexagrams sought
ways of overcoming obstacles that his ruler placed in his way. Now he
is strong enough to overcome them, but modestly refrains from
going ahead.

Notes

1. MODESTY — When the Zhou had finally defeated Shang, the
prime minister, the Duke of Zhou, expounded the new dynasty's
ideal of modesty in his address to an assembly of Shang knights: "It
was not that our small nation on its own dared to seize power from
Shang, but Heaven aided us, refusing to leave power in the hands of
those who trusted in deceit and benefited from disorder. . . . That
we underlings are now rulers is due entirely to Heaven's glorious
power." (*Classic of Documents*, "Many Knights" chapter).

2. line four — The second line of the translation comes first in the
transmitted text. I have followed Li (1969) in reversing them.

16

䷏ 豫

YÙ

CONTENTMENT

Contentment.
It is favorable to appoint officers
and field an army.

Although his situation is not as good as it should be, the person to whom the hexagram applies remains content. His contentment will not last, however. He should be using this happy time to gather strength for an advance and should not just remain sunken in false contentment.

Lines

first line/6 — —   His contentment is well known.
Inauspicious.

Since people know that he has no desire to improve himself, he is not taken seriously and remains in a low position.

line two/6 — —   He is solid as a rock.
His time will come before the day is out.
Staying as one is brings good fortune.

Like a rock, he remains solidly fixed where he is. The time for him to take action will come, but it has not come yet. Line two is the place of the subject or subordinate. He remains a loyal subordinate, making no move yet to gain advancement.

line three/6 — —   Blind contentment.
Regret may come slowly,
But it will come.

His contentment blinds him to the need for change.

line four/9 ——   From contentment
           come great gains.
         Have no doubt—
         Friends will rush to join you.

The person addressed rouses himself to action in this active line
(——). The fact that he remained content for so long inspires others'
confidence in him when he finally does decide to take action. The
three passive lines ($\equiv\equiv$) of the lower trigram represent a crowd of
followers that rushes to join him when he makes his move.

line five/6 — —   He stays as he is.
         The illness continues,
         But he does not die.

He remains sunken in false contentment. The "illness" is either this
contentment or the weak ruler with whom he is content. Line five is
the place of the ruler and it is weak (— —).

top line/6 — —   Contentment goes dark.
         His accomplishments suffer loss.
         No harm.

His contentment comes to an end. The misfortune in this is mitigated by the fact that he is finally forced to start moving.

STRUCTURE $\equiv\equiv$ 震 Zhèn   Thunderbolt (rush forward, a
                                     burst of motion)
           $\equiv\equiv$ 《《 Kūn   Acquiescent (passive, inert, a
                                     crowd)
At first he is passive (lower trigram $\equiv\equiv$) and content, then he bursts
forward (upper trigram $\equiv\equiv$). The lower trigram also represents
the crowd of followers that joins him when he does burst forward.

SEQUENCE   Both this hexagram and its inverse, the previous
hexagram QIÀN (15) MODESTY, describe people who are capable
of advancing but do not. The protagonist of MODESTY modestly
and correctly refrained from action. That of CONTENTMENT is
falsely happy as he is.

17

䷐ 隨 SUÍ

THE HUNT

The hunt.
The hunt will be supremely blessed.
It is favorable to continue. No harm.

He goes out after what he wants and gets it. The line texts tell the story of a subject who earns great merit by taking captives for his ruler. The word 隨 *suí* "hunt" refers to chasing down game.

Lines

first line/9 ——   He loses his position.
                   It is auspicious for him to persevere.
                   All who go out the gate
                        will do deeds of merit.

Although he suffers a loss of status, he can win it back and more if he goes out and tries. This active first line (——) is the beginning of the hunt.

line two/6 — —   He catches a child
                   And loses a man.

His first catch is a small one. He should continue the hunt.

line three/6 — —   He catches a man
                    And loses a child.
                    He gets what he was after.
                    He should stay where he is.

He has done as well on the hunt as he can expect. If he tried to take more prisoners, he would lose those he has. Line three is at the top of the lower trigram. It is better to remain here than to try to advance into the upper trigram.

line four/9 ——— His hunt reaps its harvest.
It is inauspicious to keep on.
By faithful allegiance on this road,
He wins glory. What harm?

Line four is the place of the officer, who wins glory by taking prisoners for his king. What harm could there be for him in stopping now? If he went any farther, he might seem to be trying to usurp the position of the king.[1]

line five/9 ——— Faithfulness is rewarded.
Good fortune.

His devotion to his ruler brings him good fortune. Line five is the place of the ruler.

top line/6 —— —— He caught and bound them
And now he himself is tied.
The king makes offering
on the Western Mountain.

He took prisoners for the king and now the king recognizes his contribution by inviting him to take part in the sacrificial feasts held in the temple of the royal ancestors. This ties him closely to the dynasty. The Zhou clan's ancestral shrine was on the slopes of Mount Qi (岐山 *Qíshān*) in western China. This top line, because it is at the highest point of the hexagram, sometimes refers to Heaven or the spirits.

STRUCTURE ☱ 兌 Duì   Stand Straight (break free)
☳ 震 Zhèn   Thunderbolt (rush forward)
Someone in a low position rushes forward (lower trigram ☳) and stands up into a higher position (upper trigram ☱). The active first line (———) chases the two passive lines above it (☵) and captures them against the two solid lines above that (☰). These represent an officer (line four) and his king (line five). Compare to CUÌ (45) GATHERING AROUND.

SEQUENCE   The subject who was mired in CONTENTMENT in the previous hexagram now loses the position that made him content and goes out to earn merit by taking captives for his king.

Note

1. "By faithful allegiance on this road, he wins glory." (line four) — The word 孚 *fú* "faithful allegiance" originally meant "captive" or "prisoner of war," but came to refer to the allegiance of a feudal subordinate and then simply to trust or belief. The passage quoted can also be translated: "By taking captives on the road, he wins glory."

18

䷑ 蠱

GǓ

ILLNESS

Illness.
Working to cure an illness is supremely blessed.
It is favorable to undertake the crossing of a great river.
Begin three days before the first day—
And you will end three days after it.

This hexagram shows someone who is faced with a difficult problem
— an "illness" — that he must deal with before he can advance. The
problem is like a river to be forded. If he starts work on it right away,
he can solve it in seven days, delaying by only three days the start of a
planned advance. The texts of the lines say that the problem is his
father's illness. He sets aside his own ambitions and goes home to
take care of him.[1, 2]

Lines

first line/6 ——   He tends his father's illness.
                       Because the son is there,
                       The sire comes to no harm.
                       Danger ends in good fortune.

He sets to work on the problem right away here in the very first line
of the hexagram. In treating an illness, the ancient Chinese used not
only medicines but also prayers and sacrifices. That may be why the
son's presence is so important.

line two/9 ——   He tends his mother's illness.
                       He must not keep on.

He sets to work on a problem that is not his to solve. He should let his sisters tend his mother and continue with his own advance. There may be ritual reasons for this apparently heartless point of view. Line two is associated with women because it is within the inner trigram in the same way that a woman's place was within the home. The hexagram's protagonist should not retreat so far.

line three/9 ——   He tends his father's illness.
                    Slight regret. No great harm.

He regrets having to interrupt his own advance, but averts the great harm of his father's death or of being unfilial. The misfortune normal in line three is here reduced to slight regret. The rest of it can be found in line four.

line four/6 — —   He neglects his father's illness.
                    Advancing, he sees trouble.

If he ignores the problem and tries to continue his own advance, he will get into difficulties. Line four sometimes has to do with being late.

line five/6 — —   He tends his father's illness.
                    And wins praise.

His filial conduct earns him the good opinion of others. Such a good reputation will make it easier for him to advance when the time comes for him to think of his own concerns again. Line five is the place of success and of the ruler whose good opinion he earns.

top line/9 ——   He serves no king or lord.
                    His service is higher.

He serves his father, his clan, and the spirits of his ancestors. Because it is above all the other lines, the top line of a hexagram is sometimes associated with the supernatural.

STRUCTURE ☶ 艮 Gēn   Keep Still (stopped)
                   ☴ 巽 Xùn   Kneel in Submission
He submits (lower trigram ☴) to being stopped (upper trigram ☶) and sets to work on the problem that stops him.

SEQUENCE   This and the previous hexagram, its inverse SUÍ (17) THE HUNT, both show ways of establishing merit in order to make possible an advance in status and power. In THE HUNT, this was accomplished by going out actively after what one wanted. In ILLNESS, it is accomplished by returning home to solve a problem there first. Both approaches are "supremely blessed" and will end with arrival as a leader in LÍN (19) LEADERSHIP.

Notes

1. ILLNESS — The word 蠱 *gǔ* refers to poison or to an illness caused by poison. It can also refer to spoilage, specifically to grain in which insects appear. On the other hand, some commentators say the character 蠱 is used for 故 *gù*, which means "thing," "business," "affair." This would make the first line: "He does his father's business."

2. "first day" (opening text) — This is the day called 甲 *jiǎ*, the first day of the ancient ten-day week. I take it to refer generally to the day on which one intends to begin something. However, the last sentence of the opening text can also be translated: "The three days before the *jiǎ* day and the three days after it." Some commentators think this refers to days that are lucky for sacrifice or other purposes.

19

☷☱ 臨   LÍN

LEADERSHIP

Leadership.
Showing leadership is supremely blessed.
It is favorable to keep on.
But keeping on to the eighth month
    will bring misfortune.

A subordinate rises from below to lead those around him. He is not
in a position to force others to follow him, but must lead by influence
and example. He must not go too far or keep on too long, lest he
appear to challenge the authority of someone more powerful than
himself.[1, 2]

Lines

first line/9 ——   He leads by his influence.
               Auspicious.

From this low position he can lead only by influence and example.

line two/9 ——   He leads by his influence.
               Auspicious.
               Favorable.

Line two is the place of the subject or subordinate. Normally, it
would be unfavorable for a subordinate to lead, but not if he leads
only by example.

line three/6 — —   Strict leadership.
                Unfavorable.
                Regret averts harm.

He is not in a position to enforce harsh orders. Fortunately, he is able to back off safely. Line three is the place of trouble or danger.[3]

line four/6 — —   He reaches a position of leadership.
                   No harm.

It is now safe for him to be recognized as a leader. Line four is the place of the officer, a leader who is still subordinate to the ruler.

line five/6 — —   Wise leadership.
                   Befits a great lord.
                   Auspicious.

Line five is the place of the ruler. Wise leadership is gentle (weak or gentle line — —).

top line/6 — —   Leadership by force.
                  Auspicious. No harm.

Only now is it permissible to use force. This top line, above the line of the ruler, is associated with conflict.[4]

STRUCTURE ☷ 巛 Kūn   Acquiescent (gentle, obedient, a
                                crowd, accepting)
           ☱ 兌 Duì   Stand Straight

One stands up from below (lower trigram ☱) and is accepted by those above (upper trigram ☷). The two strong lines at the bottom rise through and lead the crowd of acquiescent weak lines above them.

SEQUENCE   This situation can be seen as following that of either SUÍ (17) THE HUNT or GǓ (18) ILLNESS. One arrives as a leader either after going out hunting for advancement or after stepping back from the outside world to solve a problem at home. In this hexagram's inverse, GUĀN (20) WATCHING, one will halt in order to observe the situation and to avoid appearing to challenge one's ruler.

Notes

1. LÍN — The word 臨 lín means "look out over," "supervise," "control," and is used of kings and of Heaven.

2. "eighth month" (opening text) — In the *Changes*, the number seven appears to refer to one complete cycle of events, perhaps because seven steps carry one from the opening text right through

all six lines of a hexagram. "Keeping on to the eighth month" would take one into GUĀN (20) WATCHING, where exercising leadership is not advised. For the number seven, see FÙ (24) RETURN, ZHÈN (51) THUNDERBOLT, line two, and JÌ JÌ (63) ALREADY ACROSS, line two.

3. "strict" (line three) — See also JIÉ (60) RESTRAINT, line five.

4. "by force" (top line) — See also FÙ (24) RETURN, line five, and GĒN (52) KEEP STILL, top line.

20

䷓ 觀 GUĀN

WATCHING

He washes his hands,
  but does not make an offering.
Faithful allegiance
  is as good as sacrificing an ox.

He prepares to offer sacrifice but does not. Rather than making a small independent offering, he remains the faithful follower of a ruler whose great sacrifices have more power to attract the support of Heaven and the spirits. He continues to watch rather than act.[1]

Lines

first line/6 — —   He sees like a child.
                     All right for a little man,
                       but trouble for a lord.

Since his powers of observation are limited, his field of action should be limited too. This weak line (— —) in the lowest place is like a little child.[2]

line two/6 — —   Peeking out from within.
                   Be passive as a woman.

From her place inside the home she cannot see enough of the outside world to safely take action in it. Line two is associated with women because it is inside the inner (lower) trigram, like a woman inside her home. In this case, both the line and the trigram are passive.

line three/6 — —   "They watch what I do."
                     He advances and then retreats.

People look at him when he steps forward and he realizes he isn't strong enough to go on, so he steps back. Line three, at the top of the lower trigram, often shows someone in a low position who takes a step too far ahead. The one who looks at him may be his ruler.[3, 4]

line four/6 — —   Behold this nation's glory!
                    It is favorable to be a vassal of its king.

He kneels in submission (passive line — —, upper trigram Xùn ☴ Kneel in Submission) to a glorious ruler. Line four is the place of the officer, who submits to his ruler (line five). The word 賓 bīn "vassal" literally means "guest."

line five/9 ———   "They watch what I do."
                    A lord will come to no harm.

He is strong enough to accept scrutiny. Line five is the place of the ruler. He is either a ruler who is watched by his subjects or a rising subject watched by his ruler.[3]

top line/9 ———   "I watch what they do."
                    A lord will come to no harm.

He watches what others do, preparing to take action. This top line leads on to the next hexagram SHÍ HÈ (21) BITING THROUGH.

STRUCTURE ☴ 巽 Xùn   Kneel in Submission
           ☷ ☷ Kūn   Acquiescent (passive, a crowd)
He acquiescently (lower trigram ☷) kneels in submission to his ruler (upper trigram ☷). *Or:* A crowd of followers (☷) kneels in submission to him (☷).

SEQUENCE   In LÍN (19) LEADERSHIP, an underling began to exercise leadership. Here in WATCHING, he sees that it is not safe to carry this too far and that he should remain a faithful subject.

Notes

1. "washes" (opening text) — Some commentators believe that 盥 guàn "washes" is a mistake for 灌 guàn "pour a libation." Both these actions are preparations for sacrifice.
2. "sees" (first line), "behold" (line four) — These both translate

觀 *guān*, the name of the hexagram. The phrase in line two translated "peeking out from within" also includes the word 觀 *guān*.

3. "They watch what I do." (lines three, five) — This is usually
translated: "I look at my life." Gao (1947) interprets it: "I watch my
officials."

4. "He advances and then retreats." (line three) — See also XÙN
(57) KNEEL IN SUBMISSION, first line.

21

 噬 嗑   SHÍ HÈ

BITING THROUGH

Biting through.
Biting through is blessed.
It is favorable to apply punishments.

By harsh and determined action, one bites through to a shining prize. The line texts speak of biting into a piece of dried game and finding a shining bronze arrowhead buried inside, broken off there after the animal was shot. The arrowhead symbolizes brilliant achievement. Punishments are favorable perhaps because they can bite through a criminal's hard exterior to the good that lies within.

Lines

first line/9 ——   He wears fetters that cover his feet.
                    This averts harm.

His fetters prevent him from rushing forward into trouble. The solid line (——) and the lower trigram Zhèn ☳ Thunderbolt both imply a tendency to rush ahead, but in this first line it is judged too early for him to begin. The fetters referred to are made of wood.

line two/6 —— ——   He bites into flesh so deeply
                        that it covers his nose.
                    No harm.

He uses more force than necessary to accomplish an easy task. This weak line (— —) and the weak line above it present no obstacle to the advance of the strong and active first line.

line three/6 — —   He bites into dried meat
                          and hits poison.
                   A little trouble, but no harm.

Strong action encounters some minor difficulties. The poison was probably left by a poisoned arrow used to shoot the animal whose meat it is. Fortunately, there is not enough poison to do a human being any harm. Line three almost always contains an element of misfortune.[1]

line four/9 ———   He bites into dried meat
                          and finds an arrowhead of bronze.
                   It is favorable to persevere against adversity.
                   Good fortune.

This is the hexagram's most auspicious line and the line whose meaning is closest to that of the hexagram as a whole. Line four is the entrance to the upper trigram Luó $\equiv\equiv$ Shining Light. Here he breaks through to a shining prize.[1, 2]

line five/6 — —   He bites into dried meat
                          and finds yellow bronze.
                   It is dangerous to continue.
                   No harm.

He achieves some success, but will crack his teeth on it if he tries to achieve more. Line five is the place of the ruler. In this hexagram, line four, the place of the officer, is more auspicious.[1, 2]

top line/9 ———   He wears a cangue
                          that covers his ears.
                   Inauspicious.

He is punished for going too far. This top line often has to do with going too far and with conflict between a subject and his ruler. A cangue is a heavy wooden yoke, something like a portable version of the stocks, that was worn by convicted criminals. In this case, by covering the subject's ears, it has the bad effect of preventing him from hearing his ruler's commands.

STRUCTURE ☲ 離 Luó   Shining Light (shining, within)
              ☳ 震 Zhèn   Thunderbolt (rush forward)

He rushes forward (lower trigram ☳) and bites through to something shining (upper trigram ☲). The solid lines at the top and bottom of the hexagram are like jaws and the solid fourth line is like something solid on which they bite.

SEQUENCE   In the last hexagram GUĀN (20) WATCHING, the protagonist halted an advance short of trying to become a ruler. Here in BITING THROUGH, he advances again — but this time as a subject — and wins through to a shining prize.

Notes

1. "dried meat" (lines three, four, five) — The original texts of these lines speak of three different kinds of dried meat. It is no longer clear what was meant in each case. Qu (1956) suggests that the dried meat in line three is a small animal dried whole; that in line four it is meat dried on the bone, something like a dry ham; and that in line five it is dried meat with no bones in it.

2. "bronze" (lines four and five) — Bronze was both the hardest and the brightest metal known in China at the time of the *Changes*. It combined the symbolic values that we give to gold and to steel. Wealthy people held much of their portable wealth in the form of objects made of bronze.

22

䷕ 賁

BÌ

ADORNED

Adorned.
Adornment is blessed.
It is favorable for small to advance.

By making himself attractive, someone small is enabled to advance. The line texts seem to tell the story of a betrothal: A prospective bridegroom and his attendants travel to a lady's home with betrothal gifts. Though his gifts are meager, they are beautiful and he is accepted. The bridegroom and the lady probably represent the subject and his ruler. See XIĂO XÙ (9) SMALL IS TAMED, note 4.[1]

Lines

first line/9 —— His feet are adorned.
He leaves his carriage and walks.

His attractiveness can only be seen if he abases himself by getting down from his carriage. In order to be accepted by the person whom he approaches, he must avoid any semblance of aggressiveness or ambition. This lowest line represents low social position and is also associated with the feet.[2]

line two/6 — — He adorns his beard.

A superficial beautification makes him more attractive. He trims or plaits his beard.

line three/9 —— His adornments get wet.
Keeping on will bring good fortune.

Although he gets wet fording a river, perseverance will bring him to the far shore. Line three is the place of adversity. The gap between the lower and upper trigrams is the dangerous river to be crossed. He is both active and safe because this is the active central line of a Kǎn ☵ Pit trigram formed by lines two through four; this line normally represents safety in the midst of danger.[3]

line four/6 — —   Adorned but stopped
                   Are his long-maned white horses.
                   He comes not for plunder
                       but marriage.

He halts his brilliant entourage in order to show that his intentions are friendly. Line four is the place of the officer, who waits passively (— —.) for acceptance by his ruler.

line five/6 — —   Though adorned like a hill garden,
                   The bolts of cloth he offers are few.
                   His difficulties will end in good fortune.

Though his betrothal gifts are paltry, they are beautiful and he is accepted. Line five is the place of the ruler, who like a bride accepts (passive line — —) his subordinate's advance. Here as elsewhere in the hexagram, physical beauty may symbolize some other sort of beauty.

top line/9 ——   Adornment made plain.
                   Averts harm.

He removes his adornments. By hiding his light in this way, he avoids the appearance of trying to outshine his ruler. Because it is above the line of the ruler, line five, this top line holds the possibility of conflict between subject and ruler.

STRUCTURE ☶ 艮 Gēn   Keep Still (stop, stopped, re-straint)
           ☲ 離 Luó   Shining Light (shining, shone upon)

In a situation where his ruler above him stops him from advancing freely (upper trigram ☶), the subject makes himself shiningly beautiful (lower trigram ☲) and his ruler accepts him into high position (passive, accepting line five — —).

SEQUENCE   The shining prize he won in SHÍ HÈ (21) BITING THROUGH makes him attractive to his ruler, enabling him to rise.

Or else: Rather than actively BITING THROUGH, he makes himself passively beautiful and is helped to rise.

Notes

1. ADORNED — The word 賁 *bì* "adorned," "variegated," contains the element 貝 *bèi* "cowrie." Cowries are beautiful small seashells that were strung together and used as jewelry and money. For their use as money, see SŬN (41) REDUCTION, line five, and YÌ (42) INCREASE, line two.

2. "His feet are adorned." (first line) — This adornment is probably fine shoes, but it may be paint, tattooing, or jewelry, perhaps cowrie anklets.

3. "get wet" (line three) — This concept is fully developed in RÚ (5) GETTING WET.

23

剥 ䷖   PŌ

DESTRUCTION

Destruction.
Do not advance.

One who goes too far will be cut down. The hexagram shows someone falling from a height when his support is cut out from under him. The principal image is that of a couch collapsing when its legs are cut away. The word 剥 *pō* refers to felling a tree.

Lines

first line/6 — —   The feet of the couch are cut away.
                           It is inauspicious to keep on
                             · in the face of destruction.

One who raises himself will only have farther to fall. It is better to remain in a low position.

line two/6 — —   The couch's platform is cut away.
                           It is inauspicious to keep on
                           in the face of destruction.

This line's meaning is similar to that of the first line. The only difference is that one has risen a level higher — from the couch's feet to its platform.

line three/6 — — Cut down.
                         No harm.

It is better to fall now than after rising higher. Misfortune is normal in line three.

line four/6 —— ——   The flesh on the couch is destroyed.
                     Misfortune.

Disaster strikes. The person on the couch is destroyed because he
sets himself too high, entering the upper trigram.

line five/6 —— ——   A fish on a string
                         but cherished like a palace lady.
                     Not unfavorable.

Though his ambitions collapse and he is taken prisoner, he is treated
well, gaining by apparent misfortune. Line five is the place of the
ruler. The five passive lines (☷) up to and including this one are
like fishes strung to be dried.

top line/9 ———   The biggest fruit is not eaten.
                     The lord gains chariots,
                     The little man has his hut destroyed.

The "lord" is someone who is big enough to escape destruction. He is
the strong line (———) above five weak ones. The word 果 *guǒ* refers
both to fruit and to nuts.

STRUCTURE ☶ 艮 Gēn   Keep Still (stop, stopped)
           ☷ 巛 Kūn   Acquiescent (passive, weak)
One is stopped (upper trigram ☶) by one's own weakness (lower
trigram ☷). The lines form the image of a couch: a solid platform
(———) supported by tall legs (☷). The five weak lines that make up
the legs are a weak support.

SEQUENCE   If the advance begun in SHÍ HÈ (21) BITING
THROUGH and continued more slowly in BÌ (22) ADORNED is
not stopped, it will end in DESTRUCTION.

24

䷗ 復 FÙ

RETURN

Return.
Returning will be blessed.
He goes out and comes back in again without affliction.
A friend comes
    and he suffers no harm.
Forth and back on the road,
    in seven days he has returned.
It is favorable to advance.

Having gone as far as he can, he retreats to his starting point. It is favorable for him to advance because he turns back when the time comes, getting home after "seven days." The "friend" referred to is probably his ruler.[1]

Lines

first line/9 —— Return from not far.
No great regrets.
Supreme good fortune.

Since he has not gone far, there is little to regret in turning back and he has no difficulty getting home again.

line two/6 — — Fine return.
Auspicious.

He returns safe and successful from a journey. Line two is the place of the subject, who accepts a good but subordinate position and stops trying to advance.

line three/6 — — Disconsolate return.
Danger but no harm.

In the face of danger, he is forced against his will to turn back. The gap between the lower and upper trigrams is a barrier that he cannot get through.

line four/6 — — He returns alone on the road.

He must turn around and retrace his steps homeward, even if it means leaving friend(s) behind. Line four, the entry into the upper trigram, is too advanced a position for him to remain in.

line five/6 — — Forced to return.
No regrets.

His superior forces him to go back. Line five is the place of the ruler. A passive line (— —) in this position often represents a subject who passively accepts his ruler's authority.

top line/6 — — Returning, he loses his way.
Misfortune. Disaster.
If he fields an army,
he will end by suffering a great defeat
at the hands of the ruler of his nation.
Misfortune.
He cannot march forth for ten years.

This top line is associated with going too far and with conflict between subject and ruler.[2]

STRUCTURE ☷ 《《 Kūn   Acquiescent (weak, withdraw)
           ☳ 震   Zhèn   Thunderbolt (rush forward)
He rushes forward (lower trigram ☳), then weakens and withdraws (upper trigram ☷). The strong first line (——) rushes forward, then weakens (☷) and sinks back.

SEQUENCE   The protagonist of the last hexagram PŌ (23) DESTRUCTION went too far and was destroyed. The protagonist of RETURN turns back in time to escape harm.

Notes

1. "seven days" (opening text) — In the *Changes*, the number seven refers to one complete cycle of events. See LÍN (19) LEADERSHIP, note 2.

2. "at the hands of the ruler of his nation" (top line) — This is usually interpreted "reaching to the ruler of his nation." The ruler is seen as sharing the defeat rather than inflicting it. Both interpretations are possible.

25

䷘ 无望　　WÚ WÀNG

NO EXPECTATIONS

No expectations.
To have no expectations is supremely blessed.
It is favorable to remain as one is.
Improper conduct brings misfortune.
It is not favorable to advance.

Unexpected good fortune will come to someone who stays as he is, without expectations or ambition.[1]

Lines

first line/9 ——　　He advances without expectations.
　　　　　　　　　Auspicious.

He goes forward but without any idea of gain. Although the hexagram as a whole cautions against advancing, this first line is low enough that an advance will not carry him too far.

line two/6 — —　　He reaps a harvest
　　　　　　　　　　without having cultivated the land.
　　　　　　　　　The fields lie ready
　　　　　　　　　　without having been ploughed.
　　　　　　　　　It is favorable to advance.

His path ahead is prepared for him. Once this has been done, the hexagram's injunction against advancing is removed. Line two is the place of the subject, whose ruler smooths his path.

line three/6 — —   Unexpected disaster.
                    Though the ox was tethered,
                        it becomes the traveler's gain
                        and the villager's loss.

The man who tries to secure the future will lose it. The man who just accepts what comes will gain.

line four/9 ——   He may continue.
                   He will come to no harm.

Line four is the place of the officer. He may accept a place as high as this because he did not strive to get it.

line five/9 ——   Unexpected illness
                   Is cured without drugs.

An affliction that he makes no attempt to get rid of will vanish on its own. Since line five is the place of the ruler, the affliction referred to may be a weak or unsympathetic ruler. See also YÙ (16) CON-TENTMENT, line five.

top line/9 ——   He travels without expectations.
                   Disaster. No longer favorable.

This line is too high to permit an advance of any kind, even one without expectations or desire for gain. Because the top line is above the line of the ruler, it implies the possibility of conflict with one's ruler.

STRUCTURE ☰ 乾 Qián   Strong Action (solid, strong)
           ☳ 震 Zhèn   Thunderbolt (rush forward)
To rush forward (lower trigram ☳) would bring one up against a solid obstacle (upper trigram ☰). It is therefore better to stay as one is, without expectations. Good fortune will strike like a thunder-bolt (☳), bearing one swiftly forward to a position of strength (☰).

SEQUENCE   Having retreated from an advance in FÙ (24) RETURN, the protagonist now waits where he is for advancement to come to him.

Note

1. NO EXPECTATIONS — The expression 无望 *wú wàng* means both "unexpected" and "without expectations." The word 无 *wú* means "not" and the word 望 *wàng* means "look toward," "expect," "hope."

26

䷙ 大 畜 DÀ XÙ

BIG IS TAMED

Big is tamed.
He should stay as he is.
He eats without sowing. Auspicious.
It is favorable to cross a great river.

Although he is big and strong, like a horse or an ox, he should not charge ahead on his own but should allow himself to be tamed and work under someone else's direction. Together they will be able to accomplish such difficult tasks as fording a great river. He will eat without sowing because his ruler will feed him.

Lines

first line/9 ——— There is danger.
It is best to halt.

He will get into difficulties if he attempts to advance beyond this low place.

line two/9 ——— Carriage and axle part.

A relationship is torn asunder. Line two is the place of the subject, who races ahead too quickly, destroying his relationship with his ruler.[1]

line three/9 ——— Fine horses race forward.
It is favorable to persevere.
A well-practiced chariot stands guard.
It is favorable to advance.

The strong beast is under his ruler's control and may go forward without endangering their relationship. This top line of the lower trigram Qián ☰ Strong Action is apparently near enough to the upper trigram Gēn ☶ Keep Still to be influenced by its restraining hand. This counteracts the misfortune that is normal in line three.[2]

line four/6 — —   A young bullock's horn board.
                          Supremely auspicious.

A board was placed across the horns of a young ox to prevent it from injuring either other people or its own growing horns, while at the same time allowing it freedom of motion so it could be set to work. Line four is the place of the officer, who works for his lord.

line five/6 — —   A pen for a young boar.
                          Auspicious.

The boar is completely under control, penned up so it will grow fat. This line is slightly less auspicious than line four because the boar in his pen has somewhat less freedom of action than the bullock with his horn board.[3]

top line/9 ——   On Heaven's road.
                          Blessed.

He advances along the path ordained by Heaven. The solid line suggests action.

STRUCTURE   ☶ 艮 Gēn   Keep Still (stopped, restraint)
                        ☰ 乾 Qián   Strong Action
Someone in a low position who is strong and active (lower trigram ☰) is brought under control by someone in a higher position (upper trigram ☶). The trigram Gēn ☶ Keep Still is like a restraining hand.

SEQUENCE   Strength (☰) came unexpectedly in the previous hexagram WÚ WÀNG (25) NO EXPECTATIONS. Now, in order to make the best use of this strength, one must let oneself be tamed.

Notes

1. "axle" (line two) — The word 輹 fú actually refers to the fitting that holds the axle to the carriage, rather than to the axle itself. See also XIĂO XÙ (9) SMALL IS TAMED, line three.

2. "horses" (line three) — At the time of the *Changes*, the Chinese did not ride horses but only used them to pull carriages. They did not start actually riding them until later, when they began having to defend themselves against border attacks by mounted nomads.

3. "A pen for a young boar." (line five) — The transmitted text reads literally: "The tusks of a gelded boar." For reasons of symmetry with line four, I follow the revised reading of Li (1969), but the literal reading is also acceptable. Both suggest restraint of something potentially harmful and in both cases the restraint is somewhat greater than that applied to the ox in line four.

27

頤 ䷚ YÍ

BULGING CHEEKS

Bulging cheeks.
It is auspicious to stay as one is.
Those who see bulging cheeks
will want what fills them.

He has greedily consumed so much that his cheeks bulge. Now he must stop and digest it. If he went out after more, he would attract the attention of someone strong enough to take away from him even what he has — probably his ruler. By staying where he is, he will both be safe and gain nourishment.

Lines

first line/9 —— "You cast aside your magic tortoise
And gaze upon my bulging cheeks."
Inauspicious.

Someone powerful turns his attention on the speaker's greed. Only someone powerful would be rich enough to possess a magic tortoise for divination. Tortoise shell divination was the method used by the Shang kings and even in Zhou times took precedence over *Changes* divination. See Appendix B. The meat of the tortoise was eaten as a delicacy.

line two/6 —— He stuffs his cheeks.
He is struck on the neck
and his cheeks mound with food.
It is inauspicious to march forth.

Having stuffed his cheeks with food, he must stay where he is until it has been digested and his cheeks no longer bulge. Line two is the place of the subject, whose ruler will attack him if he is too ambitious.

line three/6 — —   He is struck on the cheeks.
                     Keeping on brings misfortune.
                     Do not act for ten years.
                     Unfavorable.

His bulging cheeks draw a direct attack. As usual, line three is the hexagram's least auspicious line.

line four/6 — —   He stuffs his cheeks.
                       Auspicious.
                    The tiger's gaze is steady,
                       but what it wants lies far away.
                    It does him no harm.

Now he may indulge his greed. The powerful lord symbolized by the tiger will not even notice him. Line four, the entry into the upper trigram, is often associated with movement that comes after a delay. It is also the place of the officer.

line five/6 — —   He is struck on the neck.
                    It is auspicious for him to stay where he is.
                    He must not try to ford a great river.

Line five is the place of the ruler, who will strike him if he dares to act. If he stays where he is, however, he will be allowed to keep the gains he has already made.

top line/9 ——   From bulging cheeks
                       come danger and then good fortune.
                    It is favorable to ford a great river.

Stuffing one's cheeks with food may be dangerous, but it will bring good fortune in the end. This top line summarizes all the other lines and leads beyond them.

STRUCTURE ☶ 艮 Gēn   Keep Still (stopped, stop)
           ☳ 震 Zhèn   Thunderbolt (rush forward)
Someone small or in a low position rushes forward (lower trigram ☳), then stops or is stopped (upper trigram ☶). The solid lines at the top and bottom of the hexagram are like cheeks. The four broken lines between them are the food that stuffs them.

SEQUENCE   The protagonist has grown to the point at which any further growth will invite retribution from his ruler. He must pause to assimilate the gains he has already made. In DÀ XÙ (26) BIG IS TAMED, he could advance only under his ruler's leadership. Now no advance is advisable.

28

大過   DÀ GUÒ

BIG GETS BY

Big gets by.
The roofbeam sags.
It is favorable to go forward.
Blessed.

Someone big is overburdened. If he stays as he is, he will fall. The only way he can solve his problem is by advancing, not by standing still.[1]

Lines

first line/6 ——   He lays an offering on white grasses.
                     He will come to no harm.

He makes careful preparations for his advance. This lowest line represents both an early stage in his journey and low social position. Because they did not have bronze ritual vessels, ordinary people sometimes laid their offerings to the spirits on beds of bushy white grasses.[2]

line two/9 ——   An old willow sprouts shoots.
                     An old man gets a young wife.
                     Favorable.

The old man can still produce something if he has a young wife. Symbolically, this refers to a subject's renewing himself by joining a strong ruler. The subject/old man approaches the ruler/young wife. Line two is the place of the subject.[3]

line three/9 —— The roofbeam sags.
                Misfortune.

The person this line applies to is not strong enough for the burden
he bears. This uppermost line of the lower trigram is almost always
inauspicious.

line four/9 —— The roofbeam is massive.
               Auspicious.
               There would be difficulties if it were not.

He is strong enough for the weight he bears. Line four often shows
the resolution of a problem encountered in line three. It shows a
successful crossing of the gap between the lower and upper trigrams.

line five/9 —— An old willow flowers.
               An old wife gets a young husband.
               No harm — no praise.

A burst of useless glory. Showy flowers are a poor substitute for line
two's productive shoots. An old woman's fertility cannot be brought
back, even by a young husband. A ruler in decline cannot save
himself by enlisting the help of a vigorous subject. Line five is the
place of the ruler.[3]

top line/6 —— —— He wades in over his head.
                 Inauspicious. No harm.

He goes too far, but comes to no harm.

STRUCTURE   ☱ 兌 Duì   Stand Straight (break free)
            ☴ 巽 Xùn   Kneel in Submission
He kneels (lower trigram ☴) under a heavy weight (the four solid
lines in the middle of the hexagram ☰), then stands up and breaks
free (upper trigram ☱). The hexagram is like a building viewed
from above: The four solid lines are a heavy roof and the two weak
lines are the ends of a weak ridgepole.

SEQUENCE   The protagonist of the previous hexagram YÍ (27)
BULGING CHEEKS, which was the reverse of this one, went too far
but could save himself by stopping where he was. The protagonist of
BIG GETS BY has gone too far and can save himself only by going
farther.

Notes

1. GETS BY — The word 過 *guò* means "pass." What is passed is the dangerous gap between the lower and the upper trigram. In BIG GETS BY, four solid lines straddle the gap. In XIĂO GUÒ (62) SMALL GETS BY, only two solid lines do (☷).

2. "lays an offering" (first line) — See MÉNG (4) THE YOUNG SHOOT, note 4.

3. "wife" (line two, line five) — For woman symbolizing ruler, see XIĂO XÙ (9) SMALL IS TAMED, note 4.

29

坎 KĂN

PITS

Pits.
If there is faithfulness in his heart,
   he will be blessed.
Along the road, he will rise.

He falls into one of many dangerous pitfalls that surround him and cannot get out by his own efforts. Only devoted allegiance to a ruler will bring him the help he needs. It will also bring him a chance to rise in the world.

Lines

first line/6 — —   He falls into a pit.
                      Misfortune.

This bottom line of the hexagram represents the bottom of a pit. In the trigram Kǎn ☵ Pit, the two broken lines are pits and the solid line is safe solid ground.

line two/9 ———   Surrounded by dangerous pits,
                      He seeks only small gain.

This solid second line is safe solid ground among the pits.

line three/6 — —   He comes to a place of pits,
                      Pits dangerous and deep.
                      He falls into a pit.
                      He must do nothing.

He cannot get out unaided and must not try.

line four/6 ——   A goblet of wine, a bowl of grain,
                  and extra jars of each
              Are passed in by a rope
                  through the pit's opening.
              In the end, he comes to no harm.

He is succored in adversity. Line four sometimes brings relief from
the difficulties encountered in line three. Pits were sometimes used
as prison cells and that may be the situation here. The prisoner's
friends or his captor may be passing food in to him.[1]

line five/9 ——   Before the pit is filled,
              The mound of earth falls level.
              He comes to no harm.

It is as if he is being buried alive in a pit, but the mound of earth
being used to fill it is exhausted before the pit is completely filled and
he escapes harm. In general terms, this means that his difficulties
will have an end. Line five is the place of the ruler and of success.
The middle line of the trigram Kǎn ☵ Pit stands for safety in the
midst of danger.

top line/6 ——   He is tied with ropes and cords
              And put in the date thicket prison.
              He will not get out for three years.
              Misfortune.

Prisons and law courts in ancient China are said to have been
surrounded by thorny date trees, an ancient equivalent of barbed
wire. The top line of a hexagram often involves conflict with a
superior.

STRUCTURE   ☵ 坎 Kǎn   Pit (danger, difficulties)
                 ☵ 坎 Kǎn   Pit
Surrounded by dangerous pitfalls.

SEQUENCE   The protagonists of the last two hexagrams went
too far, but were able to avoid disaster by their own actions. In YÍ
(27) BULGING CHEEKS, this was done by pausing to assimilate
gains already made. In DÀ GUÒ (28) BIG GETS BY, it was done by
boldly forging ahead. Here in PITS, one cannot avoid misfortune
nor escape it by one's own strength, but must accept both the
misfortune and then help in getting out of it.

Note

1. line four — This line and the hexagram in general may allude to the imprisonment of the eventual King Wen of Zhou by the Shang king Dixin. King Wen was accused of treason against Shang and spent two years in prison. After he was released, Zhou power increased rapidly. See Introduction, page 11.

30

離 LUÓ

SHINING LIGHT

Shining light.
It is favorable to stay as one is.
Blessed.
Keeping a cow is auspicious.

A faithful subject is bathed in the shining light of his ruler's favor. Keeping a cow is auspicious because the cow is like a faithful subject.[1]

Lines

first line/9 —— He comes on shoes of gold.
Honor him and avert harm.

Sunrise. A shining ruler appears, who will be either scourge or benefactor, depending on how he is received. "Shoes of gold" are cloth shoes embroidered with gold or other yellow metal thread.[2]

line two/6 — — Yellow light.
Supremely auspicious.

Noon. The shining benefactor's favor is at its height. Line two is the place of the faithful subject, who is passive (— —). Yellow is associated with loyalty.

line three/9 —— In the light of the declining sun.
Beat the drum and sing
Or sigh an old man's grief.
Misfortune.

Evening. What is declining is either the ruler himself or his favor

toward his subject. In either case, the subject can do nothing but just
enjoy the time that is left to him. Line three is the place of adversity.[3]

line four/9 ——   Sudden their coming:
                    Fire, death, abandonment.

Nightfall. The benefactor's favor is removed.

line five/6 — —   Tears swell and fall
                    With sobs of grief.
                    Auspicious.

Midnight. When the night is darkest, the light is on its way back.

top line/9 ——   The king marches forth.
                   Those who take heads are rewarded.
                   One captures a host of the enemy
                   And escapes harm.

A new dawn. The subject marches forth with his king and is rewarded for prowess in battle. This top line is associated with conflict
and with the beginning of a new cycle. The solid line (——) suggests
action.

STRUCTURE ☲ 離 Luó   Shining Light (shining, shone
                               upon, within)
            ☲ 離 Luó   Shining Light

The subject is within his ruler's entourage and shone upon by his
light.

SEQUENCE   The protagonist of KĂN (29) PITS accepted the
authority of a ruler and was helped out of difficulties. This present
hexagram describes the cycle of a faithful subject's relations with his
ruler. PITS and SHINING LIGHT are one of the four pairs of
hexagrams that are reverse (solid lines for broken) rather than
inverse (upside down) pairs.

Notes

1. LUÓ — The character 離 is normally read *lí*. I believe it should
be read *luó* because of the words it is made to rhyme with and
because the recently excavated Han manuscript from Mawang Dui
uses the character 羅 *luó* here.

2. "shoes of gold" (first line) — Compare the "plain cloth shoes" in the first line of LÜ (10) TREADING.

3. "drum" (line three) — The drum referred to is one made of pottery. The same word 缶 *fǒu* can also mean "jar."

31

☷☶ 感 GĂN

MOVEMENT

Movement.
Movement will be blessed.
It is favorable to continue.
Taking a wife will bring good fortune.

He begins to move again, after having been stopped for a while. "Taking a wife" may symbolize either joining a ruler or taking on a subordinate.[1]

Lines

first line/6 — —   He moves his toes.

This slight movement is the first sign of activity. He must not move too much at first.[2]

line two/6 — —   He moves his calves.
Inauspicious.
It is auspicious for him to stay where he is.

To move this much is dangerous. Line two is the place of the subject, who must not advance without a command from his ruler.[2]

line three/9 ———   He moves his legs,
But someone grabs his heel.
Advancing will lead to trouble.

He is stopped as soon as he takes a step. The stopping power of this solid top line of the trigram Gēn ☶ Keep Still is reinforced by the two solid lines that are above it in the hexagram.[2, 3]

line four/9 ——   Keeping on brings good fortune.
                   Regrets will pass.
                   "Coming and going all around you,
                   Your friends follow your plans."

Now is the time for action. Line four is the place of the officer and of movement after a delay. The friends (or friend) who follow(s) him could be either a group of subordinates or his ruler.

line five/9 ——   He moves his back.
                   No regrets.

He bends his back in obeisance to his ruler. Line five is the place of the ruler.[2]

top line/6 — —   He moves his cheeks and his tongue.

He speaks. Since the top line of a hexagram often involves conflict between subject and ruler, he may be saying something to offend his ruler. He should not.[2]

STRUCTURE ☱ 兌 Duì   Stand Straight
           ☶ 艮 Gēn   Keep Still (stopped)

Having been stopped for some time in a low position (lower trigram ☶), he takes action (lines three, four, five ☰), standing up into a higher position ☱).

SEQUENCE   In order to escape difficulties, the protagonist of KĂN (29) PITS subordinated himself to someone stronger. The next hexagram LUÓ (30) SHINING LIGHT showed him passively accepting the rise and fall of his ruler's favor. Now, in MOVE-MENT, he begins to move again himself.

Notes

1. MOVEMENT — The word 感 *gǎn* "movement" refers to actively moving something, as well as to exerting influence. It is the word translated "influence" in LÍN (19) LEADERSHIP, lines one and two.

2. "toes," "calves," etc. (line texts) — Compare the line texts' references to moving various parts of the body to similar references in GĒN (52) KEEP STILL to keeping various parts of the body still.

3. "legs" (line three) — The word 股 *gǔ* "legs" actually refers to the buttocks. Here one is probably meant to envisage the muscles of the upper leg and thighs that are used in running.

32

䷟ 恒

CONSTANCY

Constancy.
Constancy is blessed.
Averts harm.
It is favorable to remain as one is.
It is favorable to go forward.

He must not attempt to change his status, but should remain a humble subject. As long as he does, he will have good fortune, whether he stays where he is or follows his ruler on a journey.

Lines

first line/6 — — Constant in the depths.
Inauspicious.
Not favorable.

Although the hexagram as a whole advises one to remain in a low position, this position is too low.

line two/9 —— Regrets will pass.

Line two is the place of the subject or subordinate. At first he regrets being in such a comparatively low position, but the benefits of his constancy will chase regret away.

line three/9 —— He does not keep to his station.
He makes an offering of sauces.
Keeping on will bring trouble.

Line three, the top line of the lower trigram, often describes the misfortunes of someone who attempts to rise too high. Instead of making the simple meat offering proper to someone of his station, he adds sauces to it, which only someone of a higher rank should do. See PĬ (12) BLOCKED, lines two and three.[1, 2]

line four/9 ——   He hunts and gets nothing.

Any attempt at gain will fail. Line four is the first line of the upper trigram. He succeeds in entering the higher position represented by the upper trigram, but this leads to no real gain.[3]

line five/6 — —   He keeps to his station.
                   Auspicious for a wife,
                   Inauspicious for a husband.

Line five is the place of the ruler. To remain in a subordinate position is fine for a wife (subject), but for a husband (ruler) it is a poor prospect.[1, 4]

top line/6 — —   Under constant attack.
                  Misfortune.

This top line is too high. In it, he is exposed to attack.

STRUCTURE ☳ 震 Zhèn   Thunderbolt (rush forward)
          ☴ 巽 Xùn   Kneel in Submission
One kneels in submission (lower trigram ☴) to someone in a higher position and is carried forward (upper trigram ☳).

SEQUENCE   The last hexagram GǍN (31) MOVEMENT showed a subject who began to move after having been just a passive vassal of his lord. This inverse hexagram CONSTANCY shows that his relationship toward his ruler remains constant.

Notes

1. "station" (lines three and five) — The word 德 dé is usually translated: "virtue." Here, however, it refers to one's status in society. IN SÒNG (6) GRIEVANCE, line three, the words 舊德 jiù dé "old virtue" mean "patrimony," the land and title inherited by a member of the nobility.

2. "He makes an offering of sauces." (line three) — This is traditionally interpreted: "He will be disgraced." Both interpretations are reasonable, but I think the former is more likely correct.

3. "He hunts and gets nothing." (line four) — Compare with line four of XÙN (57) KNEEL IN SUBMISSION: "He makes a great catch on the hunt."

4. "wife . . . husband" (line five) — For a discussion of the symbolism here, see XIǍO XÙ (9) SMALL IS TAMED, note 4.

33

TÚN

THE PIGLET

The piglet.
The piglet is blessed.
Small should stay as he is.

The piglet stays in his pen, eating and growing fat: Someone small stays where he is and grows stronger. This is auspicious, even if he is held there against his will.[1]

Lines

first line/6 —— The piglet's tail.
Danger.
Do not advance.

This weak line (— —) at the bottom of the hexagram represents someone too small and weak to advance.

line two/6 —— He is held with brown oxhide
that no one can loose.

He is firmly held captive, but in a place where he can grow. Line two is the place of the subject, who is tied to his ruler.[2]

line three/9 —— The piglet is bound.
Affliction. Danger.
Auspicious for taking slaves.

The piglet is bound tightly for slaughter. Although the hexagram as a whole recommends that one accept restriction, in this line restriction is dangerous. Line three often describes a potential danger in acting as the hexagram suggests. In this case, the line is auspicious only for taking slaves. The two passive lines below it (— —) are like two slaves whom the solid line restrains.[3]

line four/9 ———   A fine piglet.
                                Auspicious for a lord,
                                But a little man remains blocked.

The piglet grows to a fine size. If the person whom the piglet symbolizes is a lord, he may cast off the restrictions that allowed him to grow and may begin to use his newfound strength. If he is a "little man," a commoner, he must stay as he is.

line five/9 ———   The piglet is rewarded.
                                Staying as one is brings good fortune.

Accepting his confinement, the "piglet" grows into a fine big pig and attracts his ruler's favor. Line five, the place of the ruler, is often the place in which a hexagram reaches the height of the good fortune possible to it.

top line/9 ———   Fat piglet.
                                Favorable.

The "piglet" has grown so large that he is capable of occupying even this high place. This top line often implies conflict between subject and ruler.

STRUCTURE   ☰ 乾 Qián   Strong Action (solid, strong)
                    ☶ 艮 Gèn   Keep Still (restraint, stopped)
The four solid lines (☰) are the piglet's body, the two broken lines (☷) are its tail. The piglet keeps still (lower trigram ☶) and grows strong (upper trigram ☰). The restraint of the lower trigram is strengthened by the three solid lines of the upper trigram.

SEQUENCE   The protagonist of the last hexagram HÉNG (32) CONSTANCY stayed as he was. In THE PIGLET, this enables him to grow. By the next hexagram DÀ QIÁNG (34) BIG USES FORCE, he will be strong enough to break free of his restrictions and rush forward like a charging ram.

Notes

1. PIGLET — The transmitted text has 遯 *dùn* "retreat." I follow Gao (1947) in reading this as 豚 *tún* "piglet." The piglet is contrasted

with the ram in the next and inverse hexagram BIG USES FORCE.

2. "brown" (line two) — The Chinese think of yellow and brown as shades of the same color. In the *Changes*, this color is associated with loyalty, perhaps because a glorious ruler is like a shining yellow sun. Compare this line with the first line of GÉ (49) REVOLUTION.

3. "slaves" (line three) — The *Changes* refers to male slaves (臣 *chén*), female slaves (妾 *qiè*), the two together (臣妾 *chénqiè*), male slaves without families (臣无家 *chén wújiā*), and personal servants (童僕 *tóngpú*). In this line, the reference is to male and female slaves together and probably indicates a slave couple.

34

≡≡ 大戕 DÀ QIÁNG

BIG USES FORCE

Big uses force.
It is favorable to continue.

A charging ram breaks out of its enclosure: The person symbolized has grown strong enough to break free of restrictions. This is "favorable," but it is only the beginning of a movement toward real good fortune.[1]

Lines

first line/9 —— Wounded in the foot.
Marching forth leads to misfortune.

Not yet strong enough to get free, he is wounded on his first step forward.

line two/9 —— He is faithful.
Keeping on brings good fortune.

As long as he continues to bear allegiance to his ruler, he may keep on. The ruler's strength will make up for the strength he lacks. Line two is the place of the faithful subject.[2]

line three/9 —— A little man uses force
And a lord entraps him.
It is dangerous to keep on.
The ram butts a fence
and gets his horns caught.

The ram/little man is not strong enough to break free. He fails to get through the "fence" that separates a low or nearer place (the lower trigram) from a high or farther place (the upper trigram).

line four/9 ——   Keeping on brings good fortune,
                         regrets pass away.
                     The fence breaks, the ram gets free.
                     He attacks at the spokes of a great carriage.

He breaks free by attacking at the right place and time. Line four is the place where one enters the upper trigram.

line five/6 — —   He loses a sheep from his fields.
                     No regrets.

For the shepherd, to lose an intractable ram is no great disaster. For the ram itself, the freedom is auspicious.[3]

top line/6 — —   The ram butts a fence.
                     He cannot pull back
                     And he cannot go on.
                     Unfavorable.
                     Adversity and then good fortune.

His impulsiveness leads to a period of adversity, but one which will be followed by good fortune. This top line is associated with going too far. In it, the ram has apparently waited too long and is no longer strong enough to get free. The broken last line of the trigram Zhèn ☳ Thunderbolt represents a weakening of the trigram's strong initial impulse.

STRUCTURE ☳ 震 Zhèn   Thunderbolt (rush forward, a burst of motion)
           ☰ 乾 Qián   Strong Action (strong, active)
The hexagram looks like a ram: Its four solid lines (☰) are the ram's body, its two broken lines (☷) are the ram's horns. The ram is strong (lower trigram ☰) and bursts forward (upper trigram ☳), crossing over from the lower to the upper trigram, which is to say from inside to outside.

SEQUENCE   The "piglet" of the previous and inverse hexagram TÚN (33) THE PIGLET was held in one place, where he grew stronger. Now he has grown strong enough to burst his bonds.

Notes

1. DÀ QIÁNG — The transmitted text has 壯 *zhuàng* "strong." Most commentators take the 壯 *zhuàng* that appears in the first line of this hexagram and in the first and third lines of JUÉ (43) FLIGHT to mean "wounded." I follow Gao (1947) in reading those occurrences as 戕 *qiáng* "stab," "wound," but go farther than he does in reading the name of the hexagram as 戕 *qiáng*, as well.

2. "He is faithful." (line two) — In the transmitted text, this comes at the end of the first line, not in line two. The earliest quotations from the *Changes* do not include the words "first line/9," "line five/6," etc., that divide the text into lines. It appears that when they were put in, some of them may have been put in the wrong places. For another example, see XIÈ (40) GETTING FREE, first line.

3. "loses a sheep" (line five) — Compare with the top line of LǙ (56) THE WANDERER, where the wanderer suffers the greater disaster of losing an ox. The text has also been interpreted: "He loses a sheep in Youyi." This refers to the story of the Shang ancestor King Hai, a story which has been reconstructed from various ancient references (Gu, 1931). King Hai (王亥 Wáng Hài) was probably a herdsman who crossed over with his sheep and oxen from his own land to the neighboring territory of Yǒuyì 有易 . He lived there happily for several years until he made the mistake of committing a serious crime, perhaps adultery with one of the ruler's women. His herds were confiscated and he was put to death. He gained his royal title only much later, when his descendants founded the Shang Dynasty.

35

 晉

JÌN

ADVANCEMENT

Advancement.
The Marquis of Kang was given many horses
And was received by the king
   three times in a single day.

The Marquis of Kang was a younger brother of the first Zhou king of China, King Wu, who awarded him an important fief after the conquest. This hexagram says that it is better to wait patiently for advancement to be given than to attempt to advance on one's own.[1]

Lines

first line/6 — —   He advances
      and is rebuffed.
    It is auspicious for him to stay as he is.
    To slacken his advance
      and be faithful to his ruler
      will avert harm.

If he tries to advance, he will get nowhere and may come to harm. It is better for him to remain passive (— —) in a low position (lowest line) and to bear true allegiance to his ruler.

line two/6 — —   He advances
      to sorrow.
    If he stays where he is,
      he will have good fortune.
    He will receive this great boon
      from his royal mother.

He cannot advance successfully on his own, but advancement will be granted to him if he waits for it where he is. Line two is the place of the subject, who receives something (passive line — —) from his ruler. The Marquis of Kang's mother was a Shang princess.[2]

line three/6 — —   Everyone trusts him.
                     Regrets pass away.

By remaining passive, he gains people's confidence and is granted advancement. His previous lack of advancement is no longer something to regret.

line four/9 ——   He advances like a big rat.
                     It is dangerous to continue.

He advances too boldly (active line ——), entering high position (the upper trigram). Line four is the place of the officer. The "big rat" may suggest a rapacious official.

line five/6 — —   Regrets pass away.
                     What was lacking is gained.
                     Do not fear—
                     Going forward brings good fortune,
                        it is not unfavorable.

Patience is rewarded. A passive subject (— —) is accepted (— —) into high position (upper trigram) by his ruler (line five).

top line/9 ——   He advances horns first.
                     Auspicious for attacking cities,
                     Danger but no harm.
                     Keeping on leads to trouble.

At this point in the hexagram, it is impossible to advance in a friendly way. Top lines are associated with conflict, especially conflict with a superior. Advancing "horns first" will lead to trouble. It is auspicious only for attacking cities, something that would involve trouble in any case. Once the attack has been made, a new policy must be adopted.

STRUCTURE ☲ 離 Luó   Shining Light (shone upon, shining)
           ☷ 巛 Kūn   Acquiescent (passive, a crowd)
Someone who is passive in a low position (lower trigram ☷) is shone upon by his ruler (upper trigram ☲) and advances to high

position, where he shines himself (upper trigram ☲) and is obeyed by a crowd of followers (lower trigram ☷).

SEQUENCE   The protagonist of the last hexagram DÀ QIÁNG (34) BIG USES FORCE became strong enough to break out of confinement. If he keeps charging forward, however, he will alienate his ruler. He therefore reverts to passivity, gains his ruler's trust, and is rewarded with ADVANCEMENT.

Notes

1. "The Marquis of Kang" (opening text) — The words 康侯 *kāng hóu* literally mean "strong marquis" and this is how traditional commentators interpret them. "Kang," however, is also an ancient place name and in the 1920s the Chinese scholar Gù Jiégāng 顧頡剛 realized that *Kānghóu* was King Wu's younger brother Feng, who was Marquis of Kang. All surviving ancient histories refer to Feng not as Marquis of Kang but either as Uncle Kang (康叔 *Kāngshú*) because he was the king's brother or as Marquis of Wei (衛侯 *Wèihóu*) after his second and more important fief. The histories say that he was first enfieffed at Kang, but that following the rebellion of three Zhou princes and the Shang heir several years after Zhou came to power, he was given a new fief at Wei and the new title Marquis of Wei. But inscriptions on a group of ancient bronzes, including a ritual caldron, knife, and axe, contain the name Feng, Marquis of Kang (康侯丰 *Kānghóu Fēng*). This name was apparently lost for over two thousand years until Gu rediscovered it. This suggests that either the *Changes* as a whole or at least the opening text of the hexagram was written within a few years of the conquest, since they use a title that was abandoned then and has been unknown for many centuries.

2. "from his royal mother" (line two) — The Marquis of Kang's father was King Wen of Zhou and his mother was a Shang princess. See the fifth lines of TÀI (11) FLOWING and of GUĪ MÈI (54) A MAIDEN MARRIES. After Zhou's final victory over the rebels, Kang was given a new fief at Wei, where he ruled over some of the remnants of the Shang. He can be said to have received this boon "from his royal mother" in two ways: First, he was favored by King Wu because they were children of the same consort of King Wen. Second, their mother was a Shang princess, which might have given Kang some legitimacy in the eyes of his Shang subjects.

36

䷣ 明雉 MÍNG ZHÌ

THE BRIGHT PHEASANT

The bright pheasant.
Despite adversity,
    it is favorable to persevere.

The bright pheasant represents a brilliant minister, who remonstrates with his unworthy ruler, attempting to reform him and save the state from ruin. The pheasant represents someone brilliant because it is a brilliantly colored bird. When a pheasant takes to the air, it shoots up out of the underbrush and whirrs along with great effort for a short distance before falling back to earth. The pheasant's difficulty in flying is like the upright minister's difficulty in reforming his ruler.[1]

Lines

first line/9 ——   The bright pheasant takes flight,
        beating his wings.
    A lord goes on a journey,
        for three days he does not eat.
    He goes to have words with his ruler.

The upright minister represented by the pheasant begins an effortful journey, going to admonish his ruler. He is so intent on his goal that he does not stop to eat. It is because this is an active line (——) at the beginning of the hexagram that it shows someone starting out on a journey.

line two/6 — —   The bright pheasant is wounded in the left thigh.
                      If his horse is strong, he will be rescued
                          and will have good fortune.

He needs the help of someone strong. Line two is the place of the
subject, who is helped by his ruler. To be wounded in the "left" thigh
may mean to be wounded from behind. See SHĪ (7) AN ARMY, line
four.

line three/9 ———   The bright pheasant goes hunting in the south
                      And finds a great chief.
                      He must not continue to accept affliction.

The upright minister is no longer willing to accept the affliction of
an unworthy ruler. He seeks elsewhere for a better one and finds
him.

line four/6 — —   Entering the left side of his belly,
                      He grasps the bright pheasant's heart,
                      Just as he is going out the gate.

Just when the upright minister has given up hope of ever convincing
his ruler to reform, the ruler begins to understand him. Line four is
the place of the officer, an appropriate and therefore auspicious
place for the upright minister. It is the first line of the outer trigram,
therefore he is "going out the gate."

line five/6 — —   A bright pheasant like Prince Ji.
                      It is favorable to continue.

The great Shang minister Prince Ji (箕子 *Jīzǐ*) is a model of steadfast-
ness and integrity. An uncle of the last Shang king, he remonstrated
with him over his cruelty and dissipation. When his repeated warnings were ignored, he refused to continue as a minister, feigning
madness, and was imprisoned as a slave. After Zhou had conquered
Shang, Prince Ji was rehabilitated and asked to instruct the new
rulers in the policies of the great Shang kings of old.

top line/6 — —   Not bright but dark.
                      First he flies up to Heaven,
                      Then he descends into the earth.

The pheasant falls to the ground. This top line has to do with going
too far and often refers to conflict between subject and ruler.

STRUCTURE ☷ ⚏ Kūn Acquiescent (passive, weak)
      ☲ 離 Luó Shining Light (bright, shining)
A shining subject (lower trigram ☲) has a weak lord (upper trigram ☷). The shining subject is the "bright pheasant."

SEQUENCE In the inverse hexagram JÌN (35) ADVANCE-MENT, one waited passively and was granted advancement by a shining ruler. Here one actively remonstrates with a weak ruler and is ignored.

Note

1. THE BRIGHT PHEASANT — The transmitted text reads 明夷 *míng yí* "the light is wounded." I follow Gao (1947), who considers 夷 *yí* a mistake in transcription. He suggests that the mistake was made because 夷 *yí* "wounded" and 雉 *zhì* "pheasant" were once quite similar in pronunciation. In LÜ (56) THE WANDERER, the character 雉 *zhì* "pheasant" itself appears in the transmitted text.

37

 JIĀ RÉN

THE HOUSEHOLD

The household
It is favorable to continue like a woman.

The members of a household should be passive and submissive, as a woman is toward her husband. If they are, then the head of the household will take care of them.[1]

Lines

first line/9 —— Kept at home with the door barred.
Regrets will pass.

The head of the household keeps his dependents locked up inside the house. They are held in the low position represented by the lowest line of the hexagram. But the resentment they feel is outweighed by the benefits of being part of the household.

line two/6 — — She does not go outside,
She stays inside serving meals.
It is auspicious for her to continue.

Rather than seeking advancement in the outside world, the members of the household stay inside and serve their lord. Line two is associated with subordinates and with women. It has to do with being inside because it is inside the inner trigram and in this case is also the passive line in the middle of the trigram Luó ☲ Shining Light (within).

line three/9 —— The household complains of harsh treatment.
Regretting it will turn danger to good fortune.

> If the women and children
>   just laugh and have fun,
> There will be trouble.

The head of the household keeps its members under strict control. If his control is too strict, it can be relaxed. If it is too lax, it cannot easily be made stricter. Line three almost always depicts some dangerous or inauspicious permutation of the situation described in the hexagram.

line four/6 — —   A prosperous house.
                    Great good fortune.

The head of the household is strong and the members of the household are submissive. This brings prosperity. Line four often shows the solution of a problem encountered in line three. In this case, the solution involves passivity and submission. The line is passive (— —) and is the bottom line of the trigram Xùn ☴ Kneel in Submission.

line five/9 ——   The king calls down blessings on his house.
                   Do not fear. Auspicious.

The great king is an awesome figure, but those who are members of his household need not fear him; he is their benefactor, calling down the blessings of powerful ancestral spirits. Line five is the place of the ruler.

top line/9 ——   Awed into allegiance.
                  Good fortune in the end.

The household's trembling allegiance to its head brings good fortune. Because the top line is above the line of the ruler, it involves potential conflict between a subject and his ruler. This conflict is averted by the subject's strong and frightened allegiance.

STRUCTURE ☴ 巽 Xùn   Kneel in Submission
           ☲ 離 Luó   Shining Light (shone upon,
                                 within)
The subject is shone upon (lower trigram ☲) by his ruler, to whom he kneels in submission (upper trigram ☴). The idea of being within a household is emphasized by the two interlocked Luó ☲ Shining Light (within) trigrams formed by lines one through five (☲). The members of the household are within their lord's

radiance, firmly held there by the two solid lines (=) at the top of the hexagram.

SEQUENCE   The last two hexagrams JÌN (35) ADVANCE-MENT and MÍNG ZHÌ (36) THE BRIGHT PHEASANT showed the advancement of one noble under a glorious ruler and the fruit-less remonstrations of another under a dark ruler. THE HOUSE-HOLD shows its protagonist in the household of a powerful king. He resents the restraint his ruler lays on him, but appreciates the benefits his ruler bestows. In the next hexagram KUÍ (38) ESTRANGEMENT, the resentment begins to dominate.

Note

1. JIĀ RÉN — The words 家人 *jiā rén* literally mean "house people" and refer to the women, children, and servants who made up a lord's household. In divination, the hexagram could have been applied to anyone whose relationship to someone else was analogous to that of a member of a household to its head, such as that of a subject to his ruler.

38

䷥ 睽　　　　　　　　KUÍ

ESTRANGEMENT

Estrangement.
It is auspicious to do only small things.

A subject becomes estranged from his ruler, like a wife from her husband. Even if he leaves his ruler, he must do the "small thing" of subordinating himself to a new one. He is not strong enough to remain long on his own.[1]

Lines

first line/9 —— Regrets will pass.
The runaway horse will come back on its own.
    Do not chase it.
It will see someone horrible and return.
    No harm.

The estranged subject discovers the dangers of leaving this ruler. This first line comes too early in the hexagram for a successful escape to be possible. The person whom it represents is still too weak.

line two/9 —— He meets his ruler in the lane.
No harm.

The estranged subject decides to leave his ruler, but comes upon him just as he is leaving and they are reconciled. Line two is the place of the loyal subject, within the inner trigram.

line three/6 —— He sees a carriage drag in the mud,
    its oxen taken in hand,

its men mutilated.
This bad beginning brings a good end.

The good end is that he is frightened into staying where he is. He takes a warning from others who try to leave and are caught and punished for rebellion. The two words translated "mutilated" (天 *tiān* and 劓 *yì*) refer respectively to the punishments of cutting off the nose and carving a mark into the forehead.

line four/9 ——   Estranged and alone, he meets a great man.
                  He gives his allegiance
                      and danger passes without harm.

The estranged subject leaves his ruler then meets a greater one, whom he wisely joins. Because line four is the first line of the outer trigram, it is the place where he breaks free into the outer world.

line five/6 ——   Regrets will pass.
                  In that clan's temple, they eat meat.
                  What harm could come from going there?

The estranged subject becomes the retainer of a great clan, one wealthy enough to serve large amounts of meat at its offering feasts. When important sacrifices were offered in ancient China, most of the food prepared for the offering was actually eaten in a great feast by the lord and his retainers. Line five is the place of the ruler.

top line/9 ——   Estranged and alone, he sees a pig covered in
                      mud:
                      A carriage full of men of Gui.
                  First he draws his bow, then he puts it by:
                      Not plunder but marriage.
                  Going forward, one encounters rain
                      and then good fortune.

The estranged subject meets a band of his erstwhile ruler's enemies. At first he feels revulsion and hatred but then realizes that they can be friends and the moment of danger passes. The top line of a hexagram often speaks of conflict.[2]

STRUCTURE ☲ 離 Luó   Shining Light (shone upon,
                          within)
           ☱ 兌 Duì   Stand Straight (break free, step
                          forward)

A subject stands up and breaks free (lower trigram ☱) from his ruler, then enters the sphere of a new lord's radiance (upper trigram ☲).

SEQUENCE   The protagonist of the previous and inverse hexagram JIĀ RÉN (37) THE HOUSEHOLD accepted the restrictions placed on him and remained a loyal member of his ruler's household. The protagonist of ESTRANGEMENT is more frustrated by these restrictions and leaves his ruler.

Notes

1. ESTRANGEMENT — The word 睽 *kuí* "estrangement" originally referred to having eyes that look in different directions. When a subject becomes estranged from his ruler, he begins to look in another direction.

2. "men of Gui" (top line) — Guǐ 鬼 was a principality near the Zhou homeland in western China. When the Zhou were vassals of Shang, they fought and conquered Gui, making it a part of the Shang empire. See JÌ JÌ (63) ALREADY ACROSS, line three, and WÈI JÌ (64) NOT YET ACROSS, line four. Later, when Zhou led a rebellion against Shang, the men of Gui became allies of Zhou. The modern character 鬼 *guǐ* also means "ghost" or "demon."

39

 蹇

JIǍN

STUMBLING

Stumbling.
It is favorable to retreat,
It is not favorable to advance.
It is favorable to go to see someone big.
Staying as one is will bring good fortune.

If one goes forward, one will stumble. It is better to seek the help of someone stronger and either to stay where one is or draw back.[1]

Lines

first line/6 — —   Going forward, he stumbles,
                     Drawing back, he is praised.

Rather than trying to advance, he should retreat into a subordinate position, where a superior will grant him honors. He is passive (— —) in a low position (the hexagram's lowest line).

line two/6 — —   The servant of a king faces many difficulties,
                   But not on his own behalf.

Because it is for someone else's sake that he faces difficulties, he may advance to meet them and need not retreat. Line two is the place of the subject or servant.

line three/9 ——   Going forward, he stumbles,
                     So he turns around and comes back.

He avoids trouble by retreating from it. Passing from the lower to the upper trigram is considered dangerous. Line three is usually inauspicious. Escape is possible in this case because this solid middle line of a Kǎn ☵ Pit (danger) trigram represents safety in the midst of danger.

line four/6 —— ——   Going forward, he stumbles,
                      Drawing back is the same.

There is no escape. This is the bottom line of one Kǎn ☵ Pit (danger) trigram and the top line of another. The broken lines of the trigram represent the bottom of a pit. There is danger both ahead and behind.

line five/9 ————   Just when he most stumbles,
                    Friends come to his aid.

Line five usually represents the height of good fortune in a hexagram. Moreover, in this case, as the solid middle line of a Kǎn ☵ Pit (danger) trigram, it stands for safety in the midst of danger. "Friends" can also be read "a friend."

top line/6 —— ——   Going forward, he stumbles,
                     So he draws back to someone great.
                     Auspicious.
                     It is favorable to go to see someone big.

He retreats from this dangerously high position and subordinates himself to someone greater than himself. The passive line (—— ——) suggests withdrawal.

STRUCTURE   ☵ 坎 Kǎn   Pit (danger, difficulties)
            ☶ 艮 Gēn   Keep Still (stopped)
Stopped (lower trigram ☶) by difficulties (upper trigram ☵), he keeps still (lower trigram ☶).

SEQUENCE   Now on his own after having left his ruler in the last hexagram KUÍ (38) ESTRANGEMENT, the protagonist runs into difficulties and stumbles. To overcome them, he must withdraw and seek the help of someone greater than himself.

Note

1. "retreat . . . advance" (opening text) — The words translated "retreat" and "advance" are literally "southwest" and "northeast," respectively. The homeland of the Zhou people who are the protagonists of the *Changes* was in the southwest. The Shang Dynasty

capital of China was to the northeast. For the Zhou, to go northeast was to advance and to go southwest was to retreat. See also KŪN (2) ACQUIESCENCE and XIÈ (40) GETTING FREE.

40

氢 解 **XIÈ**

GETTING FREE

Getting free.
It is favorable to retreat.
Not going forward
   but drawing back will bring good fortune.

One extricates oneself from difficulties by retreating from them, not
by trying to meet them head-on.[1]

Lines

first line/6 —— Going forward,
                  it is auspicious to go early.
               No harm.

Although the hexagram as a whole counsels against advancing, in
this first line there is still time to get through before the bar has
fallen. In fact, going forward now will bring good fortune and will
not cause one any harm.[2]

line two/9 —— He catches three foxes on the hunt
               And gets an arrowhead of yellow bronze.
               Keeping on brings good fortune.

By attacking his problems directly, he gains distinction. The bronze
arrowhead symbolizes wealth and rank. He finds it imbedded in the
flesh of one of the foxes. See SHÍ HÈ (21) BITING THROUGH.
The fact that line two is the place of the subject suggests that he takes
action as someone's subordinate. It may be this that makes direct

action possible. Compare XÙN (57) KNEELING IN SUBMIS-SION, line four. In any case, the solid middle line of the trigram Kǎn ☵ Pit often symbolizes safety in the midst of danger.

line three/6 — —   The bearer who rides in a carriage
Draws attack.
Keeping on will lead to trouble.

Line three frequently describes the misfortunes that descend upon someone of low rank who dares to transgress the bounds of his station.

line four/9 ———   He gets a toe free.
Friends come and put their faith in him.

By extricating himself from his difficulties to only the slightest extent, he attracts others to him who can help him extricate himself completely. In line four, one breaks out into the outer trigram. "Friends" can also be read "a friend."

line five/6 — —   The lord gets himself free.
Auspicious.
Gives the little people faith in him.

Someone who is strong enough to extricate himself from his difficulties inspires confidence. Line five is the place of the ruler.

top line/6 — —   The duke shoots at a hawk on a high wall
And gets it.
Favorable to anything.

Even the greatest ambitions are not beyond his reach. The hawk may symbolize a rapacious ruler. The top line of a hexagram is often associated with conflict.

STRUCTURE ☳ 震 Zhèn   Thunderbolt (rush forward, a burst of motion)
☵ 坎 Kǎn   Pit (difficulties)

He bursts free (upper trigram ☳) from his difficulties (lower trigram ☵). The idea that this is accomplished by withdrawing is not evident from the hexagram's structure.

SEQUENCE   Having stumbled against difficulties in the previous hexagram JIǍN (39) STUMBLING, he now extricates himself from them by withdrawal in this inverse hexagram.

Notes

1. "retreat" (opening text) — See JIǍN (39) STUMBLING, note 1.

2. "Going forward, it is auspicious to go early." (first line) — In the transmitted text, this comes at the end of the opening text and the first line reads simply, "No harm." See DÀ QIÁNG (34) BIG USES FORCE, note 2.

41

易 損　　　　　　　　　　　　　　SǓN

REDUCTION

Reduction.
Faithful allegiance
    brings supreme good fortune and no harm.
One may continue in this way.
It is favorable to advance.
What offering to make?
Two bowls of grain are sufficient.

Reduction makes advance possible. It is best to reduce oneself to the position of a subordinate. Only from such a position will one be able to advance. And the lower one's position, the smaller the sacrifice the spirits will demand in return for success.[1]

Lines

first line/9 ——　　Though he skimps on the sacrifice,
　　　　　　　　　He may go forward without harm.
　　　　　　　　　He reduces the wine offering.

The spirits will protect him, even if he neglects part of the appropriate sacrifice. This lowest line represents low social position. Someone who has reduced himself to such a low position may advance safely.

line two/9 ——　　It is favorable to continue.
　　　　　　　　　But marching to war will bring misfortune.
　　　　　　　　　Not reduce but increase.

Line two is the place of the subject or subordinate. From such a reduced position it is possible now to increase. One may advance as long as one does not advance aggressively ("marching to war").

line three/6 — —   If three men go on a journey,
                      they will lose one man.
                    If one man goes on a journey,
                      he will gain a companion.

Increase leads to reduction, reduction leads to increase. "A companion" could also be read "companions." Line three often deals with the unfortunate results of an attempt at self-aggrandizement. This is like the three men who lose one man. But this hexagram says that reduction will lead to good fortune. That is why someone who goes alone will gain a friend.

line four/6 — —   Reducing fever
                    Speeds recovery's joy.
                    And averts harm.

Line four often presents the solution to a problem. The word 疾 *jí*, translated "fever," can mean either "illness" or "haste."

line five/6 — —   If he is increased
                    By a tortoise shell worth ten strings of cowries,
                    He cannot refuse.
                    Supreme good fortune.

If increase is forced upon him, he must not refuse it. He either receives a valuable tortoise shell from his ruler or else divination with one tells him to increase. Line five is the place of the ruler and of success. The passive line (— —) indicates receptiveness toward the ruler.[2, 3, 4]

top line/9 ——   Not reduce but increase.
                    No harm.
                    Continuing will bring good fortune.
                    It is favorable to advance.
                    He gains a slave without family.

The time for reduction is past and now it is time for INCREASE (the next hexagram). The top line of a hexagram sometime takes on the nature of the hexagram that follows it in the sequence. The only hint of reduction that remains here is the fact that the slave brings no wife or children with him.[5]

STRUCTURE ☶ 艮 Gèn   Keep Still (stopped)
           ☱ 兌 Duì   Stand Straight (break free)

One who stands up from a low position (lower trigram ☱) will be stopped (upper trigram ☶). The two solid lines at the bottom of the hexagram (⚏) are reduced to one at the top (——).

SEQUENCE   The independent protagonist of the last hexagram XIÈ (40) GETTING FREE gained release from his difficulties by withdrawal. Now, in order to get an opportunity to advance successfully, he reduces himself to a subordinate position.

Notes

1. "bowls" (opening text) — The type of bowl specifically referred to is a large flattened spheroid called a 簋 guǐ. Typical early Zhou bronze guǐ were 15–20 centimeters (6–8 inches) high and 25–30 centimeters (10–12 inches) wide at the belly. They were used to offer cooked grain to the spirits.

2. "tortoise shell" (line five) — Tortoise shell divination was the main method used by the Shang kings and even under Zhou was considered more powerful than Changes divination. The tortoise shells used were valuable objects and were sometimes given as gifts both by and to great men. See Appendix B.

3. "ten strings of cowries" (line five) — Cowries are small warm water sea mollusks whose beautiful shiny shells were strung together in strings of five to ten and used as a form of currency. The figure of ten strings suggests a date of late Shang or early Zhou, about 1300 to 900 B.C. Ten strings is the highest number mentioned in oracle bone or bronze inscriptions of this period. By the time of the Classic of Poetry (詩經 Shījīng) around 700–500 B.C., the figure of 100 strings becomes more common. (Qu, 1950)

4. line five — Compare with line two of the next hexagram YÌ (42) INCREASE.

5. "slave without family" (top line) — See TÚN (33) THE PIGLET, note 3.

42

≡≡ 益

YÌ

INCREASE

Increase.
It is favorable to advance.
It is favorable to cross a great river.

It is favorable to make some kind of increase. Crossing a great river is the *Changes'* typical example of a difficult or dangerous enterprise or ordeal. The texts of the lines indicate that increase is most possible when one is working as the subordinate of someone greater.

Lines

first line/9 ——   It is favorable to do great deeds.
                   Supreme good fortune. No harm.

This first line is powerfully active. Not only is it an active line (——) in itself, but it is the first line of the active trigram Zhèn ≡≡ Thunderbolt (rush forward).

line two/6 — —   If he is increased
                  By a tortoise shell worth ten strings of cowries,
                  He cannot refuse.
                  It is auspicious for him to continue just as he is.
                  His king makes offering to the Lord of Heaven.
                  Auspicious.

Increase is irresistible. He is either increased by being given a valuable tortoise shell or else told in divination by one to make some increase. Moreover, the king secures the blessings of Heaven for him. Line two is the place of the subject, who accepts his lord's help.[1, 2, 3]

line three/6 — —   He gains by inauspicious actions
                     And comes to no harm.
                     Because of his allegiance,
                     On the road he commands dukes
                        by authority of a jade tablet of office.

He oversteps the prerogatives of his low rank, but is protected by allegiance to a powerful ruler. As a representative of the king, he can command even those who rank above him. Usually line three describes the misfortunes that descend upon someone who acts beyond his station. In this case, there are none.[4, 5]

line four/6 — —   On the road he commands dukes to follow.
                     It is favorable to have the Shang move their city.

Line four is the place of the officer. As an officer of the victorious Zhou, he commands the defeated Shang to move from their capital and set up a new town elsewhere.[5]

line five/9 ——   There is faithfulness in his heart.
                     Do not ask—supreme good fortune.
                     "Faithfulness is my virtue."

It is faithfulness to his ruler that allows him to increase. Line five is the place of the ruler.[6]

top line/9 ——   Do not increase
                     Lest you be attacked.
                     Do not maintain an established intention.
                     Inauspicious.

This last line is the end of increase. The top line of a hexagram often holds the possibility of conflict with a superior.

STRUCTURE ☴ 巽 Xùn   Kneel in Submission
           ☳ 震 Zhèn   Thunderbolt (rush forward)
The subject rushes forward (lower trigram ☳) while still remaining submissive to his ruler above him (upper trigram ☴). The single solid line at the bottom increases to two at the top.

SEQUENCE   The protagonist of the previous hexagram SǓN (41) REDUCTION reduced himself to a subordinate position. From there he can now advance and INCREASE himself.

Notes

1. "tortoise shell" (line two) — This refers to "tortoise divination," which is also known as "oracle bone" divination. See SŬN (41) REDUCTION, note 2.

2. "cowries" (line two) — See REDUCTION, note 3.

3. "the Lord of Heaven" (line two) — Heaven was the supreme divinity of the Zhou, who conceived of it as analogous to an omnipotent king.

4. "jade tablet" (line three) — Tall rectangular tablets of jade about 20–30 centimeters high (8–12 inches) were used as tokens of authority.

5. "commands dukes" (lines three and four) — These words can also be translated "is made a duke" and "commands the duke."

6. "virtue" (line five) — The word 德 *dé* "virtue" can also be translated "power," "status," or "station." In those cases, the idea would be that he owes his power, status, or station to his allegiance to the king.

43

䷪ 決

FLIGHT

Flight.
Captives' cries of distress
Rise over the king's palace.
A command to halt comes from the capital.
It is not favorable to take up arms against it.
It is favorable to take flight.

A warning of danger comes just in time to permit flight. If the Zhou continue their bold advance, the still-powerful Shang will destroy them. The cries of those already captured and the direct command to halt serve as warnings.[1]

Lines

first line/9 ——   He is wounded in the foot
                   on his first forward step.
                   Advancing brings no victory, but harm.

This is the lowest line in the hexagram, therefore it refers to the foot. It is the first line and an active line (——), therefore it refers to beginning something. His advance is unsuccessful because this lowest line represents someone small and weak.

line two/9 ——   Sentries call the watch.
                 Even if there is fighting during the night,
                 There is no need to fear.

Though danger threatens, a warning will come in time to permit escape.

line three/9 ——   He is wounded on the cheekbone.
                   Misfortune strikes.
                   The lord runs away alone.
                   He encounters rain and gets wet,
                   Feels resentment but suffers no harm.

He does not flee until some misfortune has already struck, but the
misfortune is not a terrible one.

line four/9 ——   No flesh on his thighs,
                   He staggers as he walks.
                   He leads forth a sheep and surrenders.
                   His regrets will pass.
                   He heard the warnings but did not believe.

He did not think of fleeing until he no longer had the strength to get
away. To go forth half-clothed to the enemy leading a sheep was a
ceremony of surrender. Line four, coming just after the midpoint of
the hexagram, sometimes has to do with being late. See line four of
GUĪ MÈI (54) A MAIDEN MARRIES.

line five/9 ——   Like a mountain goat,
                       he bounds away down the road.
                   And escapes harm.

Not only does he get away, but his flight carries him farther along
the road that he wants to travel. The five strong lines beneath this
one give his flight great power. The weak line above presents an
open path ahead.

top line/6 —— ——   There is no cry of warning.
                   Misfortune in the end.

He is not warned in time and cannot get away. In many hexagrams,
this top line involves conflict with a greater power.

STRUCTURE   ☱ 兌 Duì   Stand Straight (break free)
            ☰ 乾 Qián   Strong Action
Someone strong and active (lower trigram ☰) breaks free (upper
trigram ☱) and runs away.

SEQUENCE   The protagonist of the last hexagram YÌ (42) IN-
CREASE was a subject who accomplished great deeds in his ruler's
service. Now he carries this increase too far and must flee his ruler's
wrath.

Note

1. FLIGHT — The word 決 *jué* means "run quickly." Texts a few centuries later than the *Changes* use it in reference to running water and to startled deer. The related word 訣 *jué* means "to bid farewell."

44

SUBJUGATED

Subjugated.
The woman is too strong,
Do not wed her.

The person who receives this hexagram in divination is told to remain independent for as long as he can. If he joins someone, he will be swallowed up and subjugated.

Lines

first line/6 —— Bound to a bronze brake.
It is auspicious for him to stay as he is.
Going forward, he would see misfortune:
Captives pacing like tethered pigs.

It is better to accept restraint than to advance into danger. The brake referred to is the braking lever of a carriage.

line two/9 —— He still has a fish in his bag.
He will come to no harm.
He should not surrender.

As long as he has any resources at all, even one fish, he should not give in.

line three/9 —— No flesh on his thighs.
He staggers as he walks.
Danger, but no great harm.

Though being weak from hunger is inauspicious in itself, at least it has the benefit of preventing him from advancing into more serious trouble. Line three is associated with misfortune. In this case, misfortune has a good result.

line four/9 —— No fish in his bag.
　　　　　　　　Misfortune begins.

When all his resources have run out, he is doomed.

line five/9 —— Like a melon in a willow twig bag,
　　　　　　　　His brilliance is hidden:
　　　　　　　　A fall sent by Heaven.

He is subjugated by a great ruler and given no chance to display his talents. But since this misfortune has been sent by Heaven, it must be accepted. Line five is the place of the ruler.

top line/9 —— Locking horns.
　　　　　　　　Trouble, but no great harm.

He successfully resists subjugation. All that he joins is battle. The top line of a hexagram often involves conflict with a superior.

STRUCTURE ☰ 乾 Qián   Strong Action (strong)
　　　　　　 ☴ 巽 Xùn   Kneel in Submission
The subject submits (lower trigram ☴) and becomes joined to a strong ruler (upper trigram ☰). One weak line (— —) is subjugated by five strong lines (☰).

SEQUENCE   Having advanced his position in YÌ (42) IN-CREASE, the protagonist of the last hexagram JUÉ (43) FLIGHT advanced too far, but was warned in time to evade the anger of his ruler. In SUBJUGATED, he is not warned in time and advances into subjugation.

45

䷬ 萃

GATHERING AROUND

Gathering around a leader.
Gathering around a leader is blessed.
A king calls down blessings on his temple.
It is favorable to go to see someone big.
Blessed.
It is also favorable to continue as one is.
Sacrificing a great ox will bring good fortune.
It is favorable to advance.

This hexagram shows loyal subjects flocking around a powerful ruler. It is principally addressed to those subjects, but on the other hand it says that someone who is powerful enough can be successful on his own. Only someone rich and powerful could sacrifice an ox.

Lines

first line/6 — —   Their faithfulness is not complete:
Sometimes they are unruly,
   sometimes they gather around.
If they obeyed the call,
   they would all be smiling.
Do not fear.
Go forward without harm.

Here in the first line, potential subjects of a great ruler are not yet willing to gather around him. They should not be afraid. If they go to join him, they will rejoice.

line two/6 — —   Dragged in.
                        Auspicious. No harm.
                        Faithful allegiance makes even a small offering
                             effective.

A small amount of strength is useless by itself, but becomes effective when it is joined to the strength of someone greater. It is auspicious to join a leader, even if one is forced to join him. Line two is the place of the subject, who is loyal to his ruler.

line three/6 — —   Gathering around a leader,
                             they sigh with grief.
                        Unfavorable.
                        Going forward brings no harm,
                             just a little trouble.

There is some adversity involved in joining a leader, but not too much. Line three is the place of adversity.

line four/9 ——   Great good fortune. No harm.

This is the perfect moment to join a leader. Line four is the place of the officer.

line five/9 ——   Gathering around the man of rank. No harm.
                        Someone who has no faith in him, however,
                        Will not regret continuing on his own.

Line five is the place of the ruler—the man of rank. But the person who receives this line in divination need not necessarily join the man of rank; he himself may be a potential ruler.

top line/6 — —   Wailing and weeping.
                        No harm.

He grieves, but his grief will pass. He weeps either because he is left outside the group or because he is in conflict with its leader. This top line is above and beyond the rest of the hexagram. It often has to do with conflict.

STRUCTURE ☱ 兌 Duì Stand Straight (break free)

　　　　　　 ☷ 巛 Kūn Acquiescent (a crowd)

This shows a crowd of acquiescent followers (lower trigram ☷) gathered behind a strong ruler (solid lines four and five ━). These two lines also represent an officer and his king. The upper trigram ☱ suggests that the acquiescent followers may have a tendency to become less acquiescent and break free.

SEQUENCE The last two hexagrams JUÉ (43) FLIGHT and GÒU (44) SUBJUGATED showed a strong subject for whom it was dangerous to come into contact with an even stronger ruler. Now the situation has developed further and such contact is auspicious, though a tendency to independence remains.

46

䷭ 升 SHĒNG

RISING

Rising.
Rising is blessed.
Do not be afraid
   to go to see someone big.
It is auspicious to march south.

He rises high in the service of a great ruler. South is the direction of the sun, which symbolizes the great ruler.

Lines

first line/6 — —   Trusted and rising.
                   Great good fortune.

He is able to rise from this low position because his ruler has faith in him.

line two/9 ———   Allegiance makes even a small offering effective.
                   He comes to no harm.

Even a meager contribution becomes effective when it is joined to the great resources of the ruler. Line two is the place of the subordinate. Compare with line two of CUÌ (45) GATHERING AROUND.

line three/9 ———   Rising in an empty city.

He rises, but in the service of a failing ruler. Line three is the place of adversity.

line four/6 ——   The king makes offering on Mount Qi.
                      Auspicious. No harm.

Line four is the place of the officer, who has the privilege of taking part in the king's ceremonial sacrifices to his ancestors and sharing in the great feast that follows. Mount Qi was the site of the ancestral temple of the lords of Zhou. It lies about 100 kilometers northwest of the present-day city of Xi'an (Sian) in northwest China.

line five/6 ——   It is auspicious to keep on.
                      He ascends the steps.

He rises to the king's side. Line five is the place of the ruler. The passive line (— —) and passive upper trigram (☷) suggest that the ruler accepts his advance.

top line/6 ——   Rising into darkness.
                      Continue without pause.

Even though he cannot see what lies ahead, he should keep on. The top line is above the line of the ruler and therefore often involves conflict between a subject and his ruler. In this case, there will either be no conflict or the rising subject will prevail.

STRUCTURE   ☷ 巛   Kūn   Acquiescent (accepting, weak)
                  ☴ 巽   Xùn   Kneel in Submission

The lower trigram represents a submissive subject (☴) and the upper trigram an accepting lord (☷). The lower trigram kneels to the upper, which accepts it, allowing it to rise. The two strong solid lines (⚌) rise easily through the three broken lines above them (☷). This structure of strong lines below weak lines is analogous to the trigram Zhèn ☳ Thunderbolt, which symbolizes rushing forward.

47

☵ 困

BURDENED

Burdened.
To be burdened is blessed.
It is auspicious for a big man to persevere,
   he will come to no harm.
Words spoken against him will not be believed.

The hexagram shows someone who is burdened and restricted by
exhausting difficulties, but who is strong enough to work his way
through them to great success. The texts of the lines tell the story of a
high official who is burdened with heavy responsibilities and restricted by the failings of his ruler. In the end, he gets free.

Lines

first line/6 — —   His thighs belabored with sticks,
                 He is cast into prison's dark valley.
                 For three years he is not seen.

This bottom line of the trigram Kǎn ☵ Pit represents the bottom
of a pit. In ancient times, pits in the ground were sometimes used as
prison cells.[1]

line two/9 —————   Burdened with food and drink.
                 The red apron of high office is awarded to him.
                 He should offer sacrifice.
                 It is inauspicious for him to march to war.
                 No harm.

When his ruler grants him high position, however burdensome, he
should accept it and thank the spirits for it with a sacrifice. He should

not engage in conflict, particularly with his ruler. Line two is the place of the subject or subordinate.

line three/6 — —   Weighed down by boulders,
                    He leans for support on thorns.
                    He enters his palace,
                    But his wife is not there.
                    Misfortune.

Those on whom he depends for relief from his distress fail him. "Wife" can sometimes refer to one's ruler. See XIĂO XÙ (9) SMALL IS TAMED, note 4. Line three is the place of adversity.

line four/9 ——   He moves slowly,
                    Bogged down in a bronze carriage.
                    But his difficulties will have an end.

Line four is the place of the officer, whose powerful and wealthy ruler (the "bronze carriage") retards his advance.

line five/9 ——   In distress.
                    The red apron of high office is a burden to him.
                    Slowly, he gets free.
                    He should offer sacrifice.

He frees himself from an oppressive ruler. This is an active line (——) in the place associated with the ruler. The sacrifice he offers to the spirits may either be to ask them for their help in getting free or to thank them for it.

top line/6 — —   Held by tangled vines and in distress.
                    He will not regret moving.
                    It is auspicious to march forth to war.

He is strong enough to break free. The top line of a hexagram is above that of the ruler and often has to do with conflict between a subject and his ruler.

STRUCTURE ☱ 兌 Duì   Stand Straight (break free)
            ☵ 坎 Kǎn   Pit (adversity)
At first he is in adversity (lower trigram ☵), weighed down by the two solid lines four and five (⚏), but then he stands up and breaks free (upper trigram ☱).

SEQUENCE   The protagonist of the last hexagram SHĒNG (46) RISING rose to high position in a ruler's service. Now his high position becomes a burden to him, probably because his ruler's failings prevent him from accomplishing all that he is capable of. This well describes the Zhou people's view of their own rise to eminence under Shang and subsequent dissatisfaction with the last Shang king.

Note

1. "prison" (first line) — One ancient theory has it that King Wen wrote the *Changes* during a two-year stay in prison. He was supposedly put there by the Shang king for expressing (by a sigh) criticism of the king's conduct and was released only after partaking of a stew made from his own eldest son. Zhou power grew quickly after this and another son led the uprising that overthrew Shang.

48

䷯ JĬNG

THE WELL

The well.
If the city is changed but the well is not,
   there will be neither loss nor gain.
Going to draw from the well,
   you will not get water from it.
When the bucket is almost up,
   it will catch on the well's broken wall.
Inauspicious.

It is useless to move or improve the city if you do not also open a new well or repair the old one. The well is the source of the city's life and must be pure, abundant, and in good repair. The well represents the ruler, who is also seen as the source of the city's life. If he is no longer effective, he must either be reformed or replaced.[1]

Lines

first line/6 — —   The well is muddy. No one drinks.
                     There is no game at an old well.

The well is abandoned when it no longer gives good water. There is nothing to be gotten there. A ruler is abandoned when he no longer benefits his people. This bottom line of the hexagram symbolizes the muddy bottom of the well. The passive line (— —) suggests emptiness and passivity.

line two/9 ——   Shooting down a well at minnows.
                     The water jar is holed and leaks.

Misuse or underuse of one's capacities leads to their destruction. If the well is not used for its proper purpose, it will be made useless. Line two is the place of the subject. Under the present regime, his talents are being wasted. He must aim higher—perhaps at becoming a ruler himself.

line three/9 —————
> The well is clear, but no one drinks.
> This makes me sick at heart.
> The well could be drawn from.
> With a brilliant king,
>   all would share the blessings.

The king does not make proper use of his subject's talents. Therefore a new king—perhaps the subject himself—should take his place.

line four/6 — —
> The well is relined.
> No harm.

It is all right to repair the well rather than dig a new one, to reform the ruler rather than replace him. Line four often presents the solution to a problem encountered in line three. In this case, the solution is comparatively passive (— —): Reform rather than revolution. Line four is also the place of the officer.

line five/9 —————
> The well is pure.
> People drink from its cool spring.

Line five is the place of the ruler, who is seen as a source of life and refreshment to his people.

top line/6 — —
> The well's cover is removed.
> People have faith in it.
> Supreme good fortune.

A new well is opened, one in which people can have faith. A new ruler appears, to whom people give their allegiance. This top line is above the line of the ruler (line five). It shows a new ruler who sets himself above the old one. This presages the next hexagram GÉ (49) REVOLUTION.

STRUCTURE   ☵ 坎 Kǎn   Pit (adversity)
                      ☴ 巽 Xùn   Kneel in Submission
Submission to adversity. A subject kneels to a ruler who is a source of adversity.

SEQUENCE   The protagonist of the previous hexagram KÙN
(47) BURDENED was weighed down by his responsibilities as the
officer of an inferior ruler. The present hexagram emphasizes the
ruler's inability to succor his people and indicates that it is time to
reform or replace him.

Note

1. "city" (opening text) — The word 邑 *yí* refers to a feudal noble's
fief and to the settlement at its heart. It was also the word used in
Shang and early Zhou times to refer to the royal capital.

49

䷰ 革

GÉ

REVOLUTION

Revolution.
The day comes. People have faith in him.
Supremely blessed.
It is favorable to continue.
Regrets disappear.

It is time to make a change. He declares his rebellion and people flock to his side. The regrets that disappear are those he felt at accepting the rule of an inferior or unjust ruler.

Lines

first line/9 —— Firmly bound with brown oxhide.

It is not yet time to make the change. This lowest line in the hexagram shows someone who is too weak to rebel and should remain loyally bound to his ruler. Compare with TÚN (33) THE PIGLET, line two.

line two/6 — — The day of revolution comes.
It is auspicious to march forth to war.
One will come to no harm.

Line two is the place of the subject, who now rebels against his ruler.

line three/9 —— Marching forth to war will bring misfortune.
It is dangerous to continue.
Only when revolution has been spoken of
three times will people have faith in it.

Before a revolution can succeed, people must be persuaded to support it. Line three is the place of danger. There is danger in acting too soon. The idea of three times is derived from the three solid lines in places three, four, and five.

line four/9 ——   Regrets disappear.
                 Allegiance is given.
                 It is auspicious to change the mandate.

He rebels and people give him their allegiance. He overthrows the ruler and Heaven's mandate to rule passes to him. In line four, one enters the high position represented by the upper trigram.

line five/9 ——   A big man with a tiger's stripes:
                 Without divination,
                     he knows he has people's faith.

The tiger is a symbol of strength, self-confidence, and ferocity. Line five is the place of the ruler. In this case, it is an active line (——).

top line/6 — —   A lord with a leopard's spots:
                 Little people turn toward him.
                 Marching forth would bring misfortune.
                 It is auspicious for him to stay where he is.

The leopard symbolizes power and dazzling beauty. The broken line (— —) indicates passivity. The lord completes his revolution without further violence, as people turn toward him of their own free will.

STRUCTURE ☱ 兌 Duì   Stand Straight (break free)
           ☲ 離 Luó   Shining Light (shone upon, shin-
                          ing, within)

The subject within his lord's house (lower trigram ☲) revolts and breaks free (upper trigram ☱). He stands up into high position (upper trigram ☱) and people below him are then shone upon by his glory (lower trigram ☲).

SEQUENCE   This hexagram and the next DǏNG (50) THE RITUAL CALDRON are pivotal to the entire sequence of hexagrams. The forty-eight hexagrams all build toward them and the fourteen that follow react to the changes they bring. From the time of his first halting steps toward association with someone stronger, the protagonist of the *Changes* grew, through alternations of independence and subordination, advance and retreat, until he became the most powerful person in the state. Now, in REVOLUTION, he overthrows the king. In THE RITUAL CALDRON, he will firmly establish his own regime. The following hexagrams then describe the reactions of his subjects to their new ruler. All of this resembles the Zhou rise to power.

50

䷱ 鼎

DĬNG

THE RITUAL CALDRON

The ritual caldron.
Supremely auspicious.
Blessed.

The *dĭng* is a heavy three- or four-legged caldron, usually made of gleaming bronze, in which sacrificial meats were cooked and offered to the spirits. Since it was used in state sacrifices, the *dĭng* is a symbol of the state and of the power of the king. The hexagram as a whole deals with the establishment of a new ruling regime.[1]

Lines

first line/6 — —   The caldron is turned upside down.
It is favorable to clear out a blockage.
There is no harm in taking a slave woman
for the sons she may bear.

The new regime must clear away the remnants of the old. It should retain only people who are of low rank and can be productive. The lowest line of a hexagram is associated with low status.[2]

line two/9 ———   The caldron is full.
"Our enemies are beset with afflictions
And cannot reach us."
Auspicious.

Abundant offerings both obtain and demonstrate the blessings of the spirits. This line, in the middle of the inner trigram, represents the body of the *dǐng*. That it is a solid line suggests that the *dǐng* is full.

line three/9 —— The handles of the caldron are torn away.
It cannot be used.
The fat pheasant meat in it is uneaten
And the caldron corrodes.
Regrets will end in good fortune.

Though the caldron's handles have been broken, they can be replaced. These handles represent the officers who are the means by which government is carried out. The officers of the old regime were removed in the revolution. Until they are replaced, the benefits of the new regime—its "fat pheasant meat"—cannot be enjoyed. Line three almost always involves some kind of adversity.

line four/9 —— The caldron's leg breaks,
Spilling the duke's offering,
Sullying the caldron's face.
Inauspicious.

A support of the new order fails. Line four is the place of the officer. One of the new regime's officers either fails in the task assigned to him or rebels, bringing shame on himself and on the regime.[3]

line five/6 —— The caldron's handles and carrying rod
are made of golden bronze.
It is favorable to persevere.

Since the caldron has strong handles and carrying rod, it can be put to use. The handles represent officers and the carrying rod the king. Line five is the place of the ruler. The handles of a *dǐng* were two solid metal loops sticking up from either side of its rim. In Chinese, they are called "ears." The *dǐng* was carried to and from the fire by a rod slipped through these ears.[4]

top line/9 —— The caldron's carrying rod is made of jade.
Great good fortune.
Favorable to anything.

The jade carrying rod is a symbol of the king, who is strong enough to attempt any task. Jade's great value lies not only in its beauty and hardness, but in its imperishability as well. Bronze corrodes, jade does not.

STRUCTURE ☲ 離 Luó   Shining Light
         ☴ 巽 Xùn   Kneel in Submission
Subjects below kneel in submission (lower trigram ☴) to a shining ruler above (upper trigram ☲). The lines of the hexagram form the image of a *dǐng*: The two halves of the lowest line are feet (— —), the three solid lines above that are the *dǐng's* body (☰), the two halves of the fifth line are handles (— —), and the solid line at the top is the carrying rod.

SEQUENCE   In the last hexagram GÉ (49) REVOLUTION, an old regime was overthrown. In this one, a new regime is established. The two are the climax of the entire sequence of hexagrams. The *Changes'* protagonist finally reaches the pinnacle of power. The hexagrams that follow deal with his subjects' responses to their new ruler.

Notes

1. DǏNG — Making sacrifices to obtain the favor of the spirits was one of the most important functions of the state in ancient China. *Dǐng* and other sacrificial vessels were important religious objects, handed down from generation to generation, not only in the royal family but in every noble family. *Dǐng* were either round three-legged vessels or square four-legged ones, usually about 30 centimeters (a foot) high and wide. Many have been unearthed from ancient tombs and some of these are inscribed with long and circumstantial accounts of their origins. They were often cast for their owners from gifts of bronze made by the king.

2. "slave woman" (first line) — The *Changes* makes reference to several kinds of slaves. See TÚN (33) THE PIGLET, note 3.

3. line four — This line may refer to the rebellion of three Zhou princes that took place shortly after the conquest of Shang. During Shang, inheritance often passed from elder to younger brother rather than from father to son. When King Wu passed the throne to his young son King Cheng, making his brother, the Duke of Zhou, regent, these brothers rebelled in support of the Shang heir, Wugeng. They were ingloriously defeated by the Duke of Zhou and the remnants of the twice-defeated Shang were put under the rule of the Marquis of Kang, who was also a brother of the late king. See JÌN (35) ADVANCEMENT.

4. "golden" (line five) — In the Chinese text, this is simply "yellow." I call it "golden" because bronze had for the ancient Chinese many of the same connotations that gold has for us.

51

震 ZHÈN

THUNDERBOLTS

Thunderbolts.
Blessed.
The crack of thunderbolts strikes terror,
But the terror turns to laughter and joy.
Thunderbolts shock a hundred miles,
But not one spoon of offering wine is lost.

A powerful force strikes like a shower of thunderbolts, but leaves joy and not destruction in its wake. This describes the aftermath of a conquest. The vassals of the defeated ruler are terrified, but the conqueror treats them well, allowing them to continue sacrificial offerings to the spirits of their ancestors.[1, 2]

Lines

first line/9 ——
The crack of a thunderbolt strikes terror,
But the terror turns to laughter and joy.
Auspicious.

A powerful force strikes terror, but will leave happiness in its wake. This solid line (——) at the beginning of the trigram Zhèn ☳ Thunderbolt symbolizes the moment when the thunderbolt strikes.

line two/6 —— ——
Thunderbolts. Danger.
He loses his treasures
    and flees to the high hills.
He must not go after them.
    In seven days he will get them back.

When invaders come and seize his treasures, he flees. In due time, what he lost will be returned to him. He must wait passively until it is (passive line — —). Line two is the place of the subject or subordinate. He will get his treasures back when he comes to be a loyal subordinate of the invader.

line three/6 — — Thunderbolts boom,
Shocking him into flight.
He escapes disaster.

He gets away just in time. If he had waited until line four, it would have been too late.

line four/9 —— A thunderbolt
drops him in the mud.

He does not flee in time and is struck down by the conqueror. This solid line at the beginning of the upper trigram Zhèn ☳ Thunderbolt represents the moment when the thunderbolt strikes. Line four, coming just after the midpoint of the hexagram, sometimes has to do with being late. Mud is associated with rebellion. He is struck down because he seems to be resisting the conqueror.

line five/6 — — Thunderbolts fly
all around him.
There is danger,
But he loses none of his offering.

Though danger threatens, he continues imperturbably with the prescribed offerings to the spirits of his ancestors and comes to no harm.[1]

top line/6 — — Thunderbolts make him tremble,
he stares at them in fright.
Marching to war would bring misfortune.
The thunderbolts are not for him
but for his neighbor.
He will not be harmed.
There are words about marriage.

Though danger threatens, he will be safe if he stays where he is. The "neighbor" is his erstwhile ruler, whom the conquering "thunderbolt" will destroy. The conqueror will then propose "marriage." The top line of a hexagram is often concerned with actual and/or potential conflict. It also often deals with a new development from the situation described in the rest of the hexagram. Here the new development is acceptance of a new ruler. This is referred to as "marriage."[1]

STRUCTURE   ☳ 震 Zhèn   Thunderbolt
             ☳ 震 Zhèn   Thunderbolt

Two thunderbolts. In each, the solid line (——) is like a bolt of lightning shooting quickly forward through the two weak lines (☷).

SEQUENCE   This hexagram begins a new part of the sequence. In GÉ (49) REVOLUTION and DǏNG (50) THE RITUAL CALDRON, the protagonist of the first part of the *Changes* reached his goal of power. The protagonist of the remaining fourteen hexagrams appears to be a vassal of the defeated Shang. He escapes harm in the conquest, gradually finds a place in the new order, then begins his own rise toward power. THUNDERBOLTS and its inverse GĒN (52) KEEP STILL show two possible reactions to the conquest: terror and cautious restraint.

Notes

1. THUNDERBOLTS — The Zhou conquerors and their allies descended on the Shang like thunderbolts, sweeping them from power. But they did not attempt the almost impossible task of conquering every nobleman connected with Shang. They left most lords on their lands, allowing them to continue sacrifices to their ancestors. The Zhou king's own relatives and supporters were enfieffed with unoccupied lands between and around those of the Shang lords, where they acted as a buffer.

2. "a hundred miles" (opening text) — The mile referred to is the Chinese mile or 里 *lǐ*, which equals about one third of an English mile or one half of a kilometer.

52

䷳ 艮 GĒN

KEEP STILL

He keeps still
And is not taken captive.
They pass his house
And he is not seen.
He escapes harm.

By keeping still, he escapes harm. Conquerors overrun his town, but
he keeps out of harm's way and they ignore him.

Lines

first line/6 — —   He keeps his feet still.
                       Averts harm.
                       It is favorable to stay just as one is.

This lowest line is associated with feet. The higher lines are associated with higher parts of the body. Compare with the lines of GǍN
(31) MOVEMENT.

line two/6 — —   He keeps his calves still
                       And does not lift his heels.
                       But his heart is not content.

He keeps still as he knows he must, though he yearns to take action.
Line two is the place of the subject. Perhaps this subject's heart
remains loyal to a defeated ruler. He wants to fight although he
knows the cause is lost.

line three/9 ——   He keeps his waist still
                      And his back is laid open.
                      Danger sears his heart.

He is punished for refusing to bend before the conqueror. This uppermost line of the lower trigram often concerns someone of low rank who offends against his ruler.[1]

line four/6 — —   He keeps still.
                      And averts harm.

The Chinese text literally reads: "He keeps his body still."

line five/6 — —   He keeps his cheeks still.
                      His words express allegiance.
                      Regrets will pass.

He declares his allegiance to the new ruler. His yearning for the old ruler will pass. Line five is the place of the ruler.

top line/9 ——   He is forced to keep still.
                      Auspicious.

Even in this last line, it is not too late to stop and keep still. The solid line (——) is a barrier to advance. The top line of a hexagram is associated with conflict between subject and ruler.

STRUCTURE ☶ 艮 Gèn   Keep Still (stop, stopped)
                  ☶ 艮 Gèn   Keep Still (stop, stopped)
The trigram symbolizes keeping still because not only are its first two lines passive (☵), but their way ahead is blocked by the solid line (——) above them.

SEQUENCE   Both this hexagram and its inverse, the previous hexagram ZHÈN (51) THUNDERBOLTS portray reactions of Shang vassals to their masters' conquest by Zhou. In THUNDERBOLTS, the reaction was terror at the conquerors' onslaught. Here in KEEP STILL, a vassal who wants to fight wisely saves himself by keeping still.

Note

1. "sears" (line three) — The word 熏 *xūn* literally means "smokes" and refers to smoking meat or fish.

53

䷴ 漸

JIÀN

GRADUAL ADVANCE

Gradual advance.
It is auspicious for a woman to marry.
It is favorable to keep on.

By accepting a gradual step-by-step advance, someone who has been stopped is able to go forward. He joins someone stronger than himself, as a woman marries a husband.[1, 2]

Lines

first line/6 — —   The wild goose advances to the shore.
Dangerous for a child.
Words are spoken against him,
  but he comes to no harm.

From the safety of the river, the wild goose swims to the shore, beginning a journey that will take it to the mountain peaks. This journey is described in the lines that follow. It represents the gradual advance of someone small and weak, first to union with someone stronger, then to a position of eminence. The lowest line, a weak line (— —), shows him at his smallest and weakest, as a "child." That is why it is considered dangerous. Words are spoken against him by those who are already followers of the person whom he goes to join. See also RÚ (5) GETTING WET, line two, and FĒNG (55) ABUNDANCE, line two.[3]

line two/6 — —   The wild goose advances onto the bank,
                   Eating and drinking with happy cries.
                   Auspicious.

The wild goose moves one step farther, from the water up onto the shore. There it is happy and well provided for, like the subject of a strong and benevolent ruler. Line two is the place of the subject.

line three/9 ——   The wild goose advances across the land.
                    A husband marches to war and does not return.
                    A wife becomes pregnant but does not give birth.
                    Misfortune.
                    It is favorable to repel raids,
                        not to make them.

The wild goose goes too far. Line three is associated with attempting something that is beyond one's ability.[4]

line four/6 — —   The wild goose advances into the trees.
                    If it finds a rafter on which to perch,
                        it will escape harm.

Not only is the goose far from water, but its webbed feet are not suited to perching in trees. Fortunately, it finds a roof on whose protruding rafters it can perch. Line four is the place of the officer, who finds a place in a ruler's service.

line five/9 ——   The wild goose advances into the hills.
                   A wife is not pregnant for three years,
                   But at last nothing can prevent it.
                   Auspicious.

The wild goose finally reaches its goal. Line five is the place of the ruler and of success. The relationship between a subject and his/her ruler comes to full fruition.

top line/9 ——   The wild goose advances to the mountain slopes.
                  Its feathers may be used in the ritual dances.
                  Auspicious.

A step-by-step advance carries one to undreamed-of heights. Beautiful feathers were used as ornaments in some ancient sacred dances. When the wild goose becomes part of the worship of Heaven and the ancestors, it has reached the pinnacle of success.[5]

STRUCTURE   ☴ 巽 Xùn   Kneel in Submission
　　　　　　 ☶ 艮 Gēn   Keep Still (stopped)

A subject who has been stopped (lower trigram ☶) kneels in submission to a ruler (upper trigram ☴) and is enabled to move forward (into the upper trigram).

SEQUENCE   In the previous hexagram GĒN (52) KEEP STILL, the protagonist remained still and kept out of a conqueror's way. Now he kneels in direct submission to the conqueror, joins him, and is enabled to move ahead.

Notes

1. GRADUAL ADVANCE — The word 漸 *jiàn* simply means "advance." The idea that the advance is gradual is derived from the texts of the lines.

2. "woman" (opening text) — Some hexagrams, such as TÚN (3) GATHERING SUPPORT, speak of a man who goes to marry a woman. In those cases, the man represents a subject and the woman a ruler. In this hexagram, the woman goes to the man and it is he who symbolizes the ruler.

3. "wild goose" (first line) — Apart from the fact that it is a water bird, we do not know precisely what bird the "wild goose" (鴻 *hóng*) is. Moreover, since Chinese does not usually distinguish between singular and plural, the text may be referring to a flock of birds rather than just one.

4. "not to make them" (line three) — This clause is supplied from context. See MÉNG (4) THE YOUNG SHOOT, top line, where it is included in the text.

5. "ritual dances" (top line) — Feather adornments are common among both East Asian and Amerindian shamans. For the wild goose's feathers to be used in the ritual dances is an honor similar to the officer's being invited to take part in his ruler's sacrificial feasts. See SUÍ (17) THE HUNT, top line, and SHĒNG (46) RISING, line four.

54

歸妹 GUĪ MÈI

A MAIDEN
MARRIES

A maiden marries.
Marching to war brings misfortune.
It is not favorable.

It is favorable to advance humbly and peacefully, like a young girl going to be married. It is not favorable to advance boldly, as if to war. The texts of the lines tell the story of a girl who is married as a lowly concubine but rises to the high position of full wife.

Lines

first line/9 —— The maiden marries as a concubine.
Though she walks with a limp,
It is auspicious for her to march forth.

Being concubine rather than full wife is a deficiency like lameness, but in this case the deficiency is an advantage. Only someone in a low position like that of concubine can advance unopposed. The lowest line of a hexagram symbolizes low position.[1]

line two/9 —— She sees dimly.
It is favorable for her to remain in seclusion.

Since she cannot see what lies ahead, she should stay where she is and not marry. Line two, in the middle of the inner trigram, often has to do with being inside of something—in this case, a maiden's home.

line three/6 — —   The maiden marries as principal wife—
                    She is sent back to return as a concubine.

Ambition leads to a fall. Rather than trying to start at the top, one
must start at the bottom and work upward. Line three often refers to
someone who overreaches himself.[1]

line four/9 ——   The maiden's marriage is delayed.
                    A late marriage comes in its time.

Line four often speaks of delay. In this case, the delay is auspicious.
The solid line (——) and active upper trigram Zhèn ☳ Thunderbolt both suggest action.

line five/6 — —   When King Diyi gave his sister in marriage,
                    One of the concubines was more beautiful
                       than the lady bride.
                    The moon comes full.
                    Supremely auspicious.

In time, the humble concubine will be exalted. Her moon will swell
from new to full. Diyi was the second-last Shang king of China. It is
said that he gave two successive lords of Zhou brides from the royal
clans. The lord of Zhou rose to be an important vassal of the king,
just as the concubine here rises to become principal wife. Line five is
the place of the ruler. The receptive broken line (— —) shows the
lord of Zhou receiving the king's gift and the concubine receiving
the lord of Zhou's favor. Compare TÀI (11) FLOWING, line five.[1, 2]

top line/6 — —   The bride offers a box
                       that is empty.
                    The groom sacrifices a sheep
                       that does not bleed.
                    Unfavorable.

Marriage is no longer favorable. The bride is barren and the groom
has no seed. The box and the sheep were religious offerings made as
part of the ancient wedding ceremony.

STRUCTURE   ☳ 震 Zhèn   Thunderbolt (rush forward)
            ☱ 兌 Duì   Stand Straight (break free, step
                                forward)
The concubine stands up from low position (lower trigram ☱) and
rushes forward into high position (upper trigram ☳).

SEQUENCE   This hexagram and its inverse, the previous hexagram JIÀN (53) GRADUAL ADVANCE, show a subject of the defeated Shang finding a place in the new order. In GRADUAL ADVANCE, he submits and rises step by step. In A MAIDEN MARRIES, he starts in a low position and is elevated to a high one.

Notes

1. "concubine" (first line, lines three and five) — When a woman went to be married, she was accompanied by a train of bridesmaids and bridesmen, some of whom would remain with her as servants or companions for herself and her new husband. The women were called 娣 *dì* "younger sisters." This is the word translated "concubine."

2. "sister" (line five) — The word 妹 *mèi* "sister" refers specifically to a younger sister. In fact, however, the woman referred to here was probably a distant cousin of the king, rather than his sister. In Shang times, all members of a family in the same generation were thought of as brothers and sisters.

55

〓〓 豐 　　　　　　　　FĒNG

ABUNDANCE

Abundance.
Blessed.
A king calls down blessings.
Do not grieve.
It is good to be in the light of the noon sun.

One enters the service of a shining king, who calls down the blessings of his ancestors upon his subjects. His abundant wealth and power allow him to look after his subjects and to provide them with opportunities to display their talents.[1]

Lines

first line/9 —— 　He meets his true lord.
　　　　　　　　There will be a week without harm.
　　　　　　　　Going forward, he will rise.

This lowest line shows someone in a low position entering into an association that will bring him a period of safety and allow him to rise. The "week" referred to is the ancient ten-day week.[2]

line two/6 —— 　　So great a canopy
　　　　　　　　That a lamp can be seen at noon.
　　　　　　　　Going forward, he is met with suspicion,
　　　　　　　　But expressing allegiance brings good fortune.

The king provides such shelter that even the little subject's weak light can be seen. At first those around the king are suspicious of the newcomer, but his clear declaration of allegiance wins their acceptance.[3, 4]

line three/9 ——— So many banners
That there is darkness at noon.
Though his right arm is broken,
He comes to no harm.

The canopy's welcome shade becomes the oppressive darkness of a host of battle flags. He does not join the ruler freely, but is made to join him by force. The harm he suffers is not permanent, but while his right arm is broken he is unable to serve the ruler properly and rise in his service.[3, 5]

line four/9 ——— So great a canopy
That a lamp can be seen at noon.
He meets his true lord.
Auspicious.

The powerful lord provides a shelter under which his subjects can display their talents. Line four is the place of the officer. As the first line of the upper trigram, it represents entry into high position.[3, 4]

line five/6 —— His inner brilliance
Wins honor and praise.
Auspicious.

The subject's talents are recognized and rewarded by his ruler. Line five is the place of the ruler. The passive line (— —) suggests the ruler's acceptance of his subject.

top line/6 —— Enormous palace,
Shaded home.
Peek in at the gate—
It is silent, unpeopled.
No one is seen there for three years.

This is the only line in which the king's palace is a really inauspicious place. The week of safety promised in the first line comes to an end. The strength of the upper trigram Zhèn ☳ Thunderbolt peters out in this second weak line. Since the top line of a hexagram often involves conflict, perhaps the palace's inhabitants have gone to war.[3]

STRUCTURE ☳ 震 Zhèn   Thunderbolt (rush forward)
           ☲ 離 Luó   Shining Light (shining, shone upon)

The bright lower trigram represents someone both brilliant in his own right and shone upon by a ruler who is like the sun. He rushes forward into high position (upper trigram ☳).

SEQUENCE   This hexagram is paired with its inverse LǓ (56) THE WANDERER. In ABUNDANCE, the protagonist finds his "true lord" right away. In THE WANDERER, he is forced to wander on until he finds him.

Notes

1. "Do not grieve." (opening text) — I am not certain what one is not to grieve over. Perhaps it is the possibility that this good fortune will not last. More likely it is the demise of one's previous ruler.

2. "a week without harm" (first line) — Shang Dynasty oracle bone divination records indicate that the Shang kings divined the auspiciousness of each week on the last day of the one before it. The phrase used here is very similar to that used in the oracle bone inscriptions. This suggests either an early Zhou (or earlier) date for this hexagram or else the carryover of Shang divination traditions into Zhou.

3. ABUNDANCE, "great" (lines two and four), "many" (line three), "enormous" (top line) — All these translate the same word 豐 fēng.

4. "lamp" (lines two and four) — The transmitted text has 斗 dǒu "dipper," referring to the constellation. One Han Dynasty version of the text has 主, which Gao (1947) says should be read zhǔ "wick," "lamp." This would have been an oil lamp or tallow candle.

5. "darkness" (line three) — The transmitted text has 沫 mèi "weak light," which most traditional commentators say refers to the minor stars of the dipper (see note 2). Several ancient versions of the text have 昧 mèi "dim," "dark," which is the reading I use here.

56

 LǓ

THE WANDERER

The wanderer.
Small is blessed.
It is auspicious to keep wandering.

The wanderer's journey will end only when he finds a good place to stay. He is a little man who seeks a ruler and a home. He has not found them yet, but will if he keeps looking.

Lines

first line/6 — —   He travels meagerly.
　　　　　　　　This is what procures disaster.

He travels either not far enough or without sufficient money and provisions. The opening text says small is blessed, but this is too small. Extreme smallness is suggested by the line's low position and by its being a weak line (— —).

line two/6 — —   The wanderer reaches a stopping place.
　　　　　　　　He keeps his possessions,
　　　　　　　　Gains a young servant,
　　　　　　　　And stays.

The wanderer finds a safe and comfortable place to stop for a while. No one robs him and he is given a servant. Line two is the place of the subordinate.

line three/9 ——   The wanderer's stopping place burns.
　　　　　　　　He loses his young servant.
　　　　　　　　It is dangerous to remain as one is.

The respite from his wanderings proves only temporary. Line three is almost always inauspicious.

line four/9 ——   Ending his wanderings,
                        He gains possessions and an axe.
                        "But my heart is not content."

He finds a home, but remains dissatisfied. Line four is the place of the officer, whose ruler gives him a weapon and wealth. He remains dissatisfied either because he wants higher rank or because he is thinking of his previous ruler.[1]

line five/6 — —   He shoots at a pheasant.
                        Though his first arrow misses its mark,
                        He ends with praise and command.

The wanderer's talents are recognized and rewarded by his ruler. To shoot at a pheasant means to seek high office. The brightly colored pheasant symbolizes a brilliant minister.[2]

top line/9 ——   The bird's nest burns.
                        The wanderer's laughter
                        Becomes a howl of despair.
                        He loses an ox from his fields.
                        Misfortune.

What seemed a safe haven is destroyed. The bird builds his nest in too high and exposed a position. The wanderer seeks too high a rank. The top line of a hexagram is above the line of the ruler (line five) and therefore often has to do with conflict between a subject and his ruler.[3]

STRUCTURE ☲ 離 Luó   Shining Light (shining, within)
           ☶ 艮 Gēn   Keep Still (stop, stopped)
The wanderer does not stop (lower trigram ☶) until he finds a place where he can shine (upper trigram ☲). The place where he first stops (☶) goes up in flames (☲).

SEQUENCE   The protagonist of FĒNG (55) ABUNDANCE was a vassal of the defeated Shang who found a place in the new Zhou order right away. The protagonist of the inverse hexagram THE WANDERER is forced to leave the first place he finds and wander on until he finds a more permanent one. Many of the dispossessed Shang became wandering merchants after their defeat.

Notes

1. "But my heart is not content." (line four) — See GĒN (52) KEEP STILL, line two.

2. "pheasant" (line five) — See MÍNG ZHÌ (36) THE BRIGHT PHEASANT.

3. "loses an ox from his fields" (top line) — See DÀ QIÁNG (34) BIG USES FORCE, note 3.

57

XÙN

KNEELING
IN SUBMISSION

Kneeling in submission.
Small is blessed.
It is favorable to go forward.
It is favorable to go to see someone big.

Someone small kneels in submission to someone big. Far from being a misfortune, this is blessed. By joining someone bigger, he is enabled to get ahead.[1]

Lines

first line/6 — —　　He advances
　　　　　　　　　and then retreats.
　　　　　　　　It is favorable to remain a common soldier.

By retreating, he avoids defeat. He should remain a common soldier because if he does not he will be destroyed. This lowest line symbolizes low rank. The broken or passive (— —) line suggests retreat.[2]

line two/9 ——　　He kneels before the royal couch
　　　　　　　　And is consecrated by the scribes and shamans.
　　　　　　　　Auspicious.
　　　　　　　　He comes to no harm.

He submits to the king and is consecrated to this service. Line two is the place of the subject or subordinate. Because this suits the overall meaning of the hexagram so well, the line is auspicious.[3, 4]

line three/9 —— Disconsolate,
                      he kneels in submission.
                  Trouble.

He is forced to submit against his will. Such misfortune is normal in
line three.

line four/6 — — Regrets will pass.
                   He makes a great catch on the hunt.

At first he regrets having to submit, but in the end he profits by it. He
goes hunting with his new ruler and makes a great catch: of animals,
of men, or of increased status. Line four is the place of the officer.[5]

line five/9 —— Keeping on brings good fortune.
                  Regrets will pass.
                  Not at all unfavorable.
                  No beginning but a good end.
                  He submits three days before the seventh day
                  And three days after it he has good fortune.

Though at first submission appears to be a disaster, it will prove
beneficial in the end. "Seventh day" refers to the day called 庚 *gēng*,
the seventh day of the ancient ten-day week. He submits at midweek,
before he is forced to, and has success by week's end.[6]

top line/9 —— He kneels before the royal couch
                 And loses his possessions and his axe.
                 Keeping on brings misfortune.

He is brought low when he tries to put himself above his ruler, who is
represented by line five. The wealth and the weapon that the ruler
once gave him are taken away.[3, 7]

STRUCTURE ☴ 巽 Xùn   Kneel in Submission
                 ☴ 巽 Xùn   Kneel in Submission
Each trigram shows a weak subject (weak line — —) kneeling beneath a strong ruler (strong lines ══).

SEQUENCE   The protagonist of the last hexagram LǙ (56)
THE WANDERER wandered about in search of a suitable ruler. In
this hexagram, he is forced to end his search, whether he chooses to
or not. In the sequence, this hexagram represents both the depth of
powerlessness for the vassal of defeated Shang and the beginning of
a rise toward power in the new Zhou regime.

Notes

1. KNEELING IN SUBMISSION — The principal meaning traditionally given to the character 巽 *xùn* is "submissive" or "submit." Ancient forms of the character, especially the Shang form 𢀒 , are thought to resemble two kneeling figures.

2. "common soldier" (first line) — See also LǙ (10) TREADING, line three.

3. "royal couch" (line two, top line) — The accepted meaning of the word 牀 *chuáng* is "bed." I call it "royal couch" because of its context both here and in PŌ (23) DESTRUCTION, lines one, two, and four.

4. "consecrated" (line two) — Where the transmitted text has 紛 *fēn* "many," I follow Gao (1947) in reading 釁 *xìn* "consecrated." Many things, including captured weapons, sacrificial vessels, and even men could be daubed with the blood of a sacrificed animal to remove evil influences from them.

5. "makes a great catch" (line four) — This is literally "catches three kinds." Various commentators suggest this means three kinds of animals, three grades of men, or three steps in rank. Compare SHĪ (7) ARMY, line two, and GǍN (31) MOVEMENT, line four.

6. "three days before the seventh day" (line five) — For a similar phrase involving the first day, see GǓ (18) ILLNESS, note 2.

7. "axe" (top line) — See also LǙ (56) THE WANDERER, line four.

58

☱ 兑

DUÌ

STAND STRAIGHT

> Stand straight.
> Standing up straight will be blessed.
> It is favorable to continue.

A subject rises to his feet. As long as he avoids giving offense to his ruler, this will be the beginning of a further rise.[1]

Lines

first line/9 —— Standing up in response.
                     Auspicious.

He stands up from his low position in response to his ruler's call.

line two/9 —— Standing up in allegiance.
                     Auspicious.
                     Regrets will pass.

Line two is the place of the subject, who stands up ready to do what his ruler asks. Though he rises to his feet, he is still a loyal subject. His fears that standing up may be dangerous are unjustified. His regrets that he must remain loyal will pass.

line three/6 — — He comes and stands up.
                     Inauspicious.

He boldly rises to his feet right in front of his ruler and is struck down. Line three, at the top of the lower trigram, often shows the misfortunes of someone of low rank who tries to rise too high.

line four/9 ——   Before talk of standing up has been settled,
                          The great affliction that gave rise to it is cured.

The ruler corrects something that made his subject think of moving toward independence.[2]

line five/9 ——   Allegiance is destroyed.

Line five is the place of the ruler. If the subject stands up here, he will destroy all good faith between himself and his ruler.

top line/6 — —   Dragged to his feet.

This top line is associated with conflict between subject and ruler.

STRUCTURE ☱ 兌 Duì   Stand Straight (break free, step forward)
              ☱ 兌 Duì   Stand Straight
Two strong lines stand up through the weak line above them.

SEQUENCE   A subject who has been KNEELING IN SUBMISSION (XÙN, 57) rises to his feet. In the next hexagram HUÀN (59) THE FLOOD, he will be swept off his feet and up to high position.

Notes

1. STAND STRAIGHT — Traditional commentators say that 兌 *duì* here has the meaning 悅 *yuè* "pleasure." Gao (1947) and Li (1969) read it as 說 *shuō* "speak." The word 兌 *duì* itself means "straight," "connecting," or "exchange." I derive the meaning "stand straight" from context, especially the hexagram's pairing with XÙN (57) KNEELING IN SUBMISSION.

2. "affliction" (line four) — See YÙ (16) CONTENTMENT, line five. WÚ WÀNG (25) NO EXPECTATIONS, line five, and SǓN (41) REDUCTION, line four.

59

☵ 渙　　　　　　HUÀN

THE FLOOD

The flood.
Being swept by a flood is blessed.
A king calls down blessings to his temple.
It is favorable to cross a great river.
It is favorable to keep on.

What seems like disaster proves to be a blessing. The protagonist is inundated by a rush of water, an irresistible and apparently destructive force. But this destructive force proves beneficial, sweeping him up to a height he could not have reached on his own. A great king uses his power to benefit his subjects. "To cross a great river" is to undertake some difficult and/or dangerous task or ordeal.[1, 2]

Lines

first line/6 — —　　He can be rescued if his horse is strong.
　　　　　　　　　Auspicious.

He is in difficulties and needs help. This bottom line of the trigram Kǎn ☵ Pit (difficulties) shows someone in the depths of difficulties.[3]

line two/9 ——　　The flood sweeps his boat ahead.
　　　　　　　　　Regrets will pass.

The apparent disaster of the flood is really a blessing. He is well placed to make the most of the situation. Line two is the place of the subject, who is aided by his ruler.[4]

line three/6 — —   Swept away by the flood.
                    No regrets.

He is swept away, but not to disaster. Line three is usually inauspicious, but here the inauspiciousness is only apparent.

line four/6 — —   The flood sweeps him from the herd.
                    Supreme good fortune.
                    It sweeps him up onto a hilltop,
                    High beyond expectation.

Line four is the place of the high officer and the entry into the higher world represented by the upper trigram.

line five/9 ———   Flooded with sweat
                       at the Great Command,
                    He is swept up to the residence of the king,
                       but comes to no harm.

When the king commands his presence at the palace, he is terrified. But he need not be, for his submissiveness will please the king. Line five is the place of the ruler.

top line/9 ———   The flood sweeps sorrow far away.
                    He comes to no harm.

The flood at first seems terrible, but as it recedes his fear subsides with the water level.[5]

STRUCTURE ☴ 巽 Xùn   Kneel in Submission
           ☵ 坎 Kǎn   Pit (difficulties)
Someone small is in difficulties (lower trigram ☵), but submits to someone greater (upper trigram ☴) and is borne ahead (into the upper trigram). Lines two through four form the trigram Zhèn ☳ Thunderbolt (rush forward). This helps to move the small person ahead.

SEQUENCE   From the abject submission of XÙN (57) KNEELING IN SUBMISSION, the protagonist rose to his feet in DUÌ (58) STAND STRAIGHT, seeking higher rank. This exposes him to the direct interest of the king and therefore to danger. A flood of royal power sweeps him off his feet, but deposits him in the high place he sought.

Notes

1. THE FLOOD — The word 渙 *huàn* means "flood" in the sense of a great rush of water. It also means to sweep apart or disperse.

2. "calls down blessings" (opening text) — The king calls on the powerful spirits of his ancestors to aid his cause and that of his followers. The text reads literally: "King calls to temple." This refers directly to the spirits' coming to the temple and only indirectly to the blessings they bring. See also JĪA RÉN (37) THE HOUSEHOLD, line five, CUÌ (45) GATHERING AROUND, FĒNG (55) ABUNDANCE.

3. "rescued" (first line) — See also MÍNG ZHÌ (36) THE BRIGHT PHEASANT.

4. "boat" (line two) — With Li (1969) I read 杭 *háng* "boat" for 机 *jĭ* "table."

5. "sweeps sorrow far away" (top line) — See also XIǍO XÙ (9) SMALL IS TAMED. With Li (1969) I read 恤 *xù* "sorrow" for 血 *xuè* "blood."

60

節   JÍE

RESTRAINT

Restraint.
Restraint is blessed.
But when restraint is bitter,
   do not persevere in it.

Restraint is advisable under most circumstances, but not when it is painful or when it goes so far as to be total immobility.[1]

Lines

first line/9 ———   He does not go out his door.
                   Avoids harm.

The first line is the doorway to the hexagram. As the lowest line, it represents someone weak and small, for whom entering the outside world would be dangerous.[2]

line two/9 ———   He does not go out his gate.
                   Inauspicious.

It is time for him to somewhat relax his restraint. Line two is the place of the subject, who cannot serve his ruler if he does not act.[2]

line three/6 —— ——   Lack of restraint
                      Brings sad lamentation,
                      But no harm.

The consequences of not restraining oneself are bad but not disastrous. This top line of the lower trigram represents a subject who oversteps his bounds.

line four/6 — —　　Settled restraint.
　　　　　　　　　　Blessed.

He is used to restraining himself and therefore finds it easy. Such easy restraint is extremely auspicious. Line four is the place of the officer and the entry into the upper trigram. He rises to serve his ruler as an officer. The line's settled quality is related to its being passive (— —) and in the middle of a Gēn ☶ Keep Still trigram formed by lines three through five.

line five/9 ———　　Strict restraint.
　　　　　　　　　　Auspicious.
　　　　　　　　　　Going forward, he will rise.

Strict restraint permits him to rise. Line five is the place of the ruler; the solid line is a solid restraint. He restrains himself from offending against his ruler and is helped to rise to a position of eminence.[3]

top line/6 — —　　Bitter restraint.
　　　　　　　　　　To continue brings misfortune.
　　　　　　　　　　Regrets will pass.

Such strict restraint is not advisable and should be abandoned. The uneasiness one feels at first will later vanish. This top line passes beyond the restraint suggested by the rest of the hexagram.

STRUCTURE ☵ 坎 Kǎn　　Pit (difficulties)
　　　　　　☱ 兑 Duì　　Stand Straight
Standing up (lower trigram ☱) will lead to difficulties (upper trigram ☵), so restraint is best. Compare TÚN (3) GATHERING SUPPORT, in which rushing forward (☳) leads to difficulties (☵).

SEQUENCE　　Having been carried forward to comparatively high position in the previous hexagram HUÀN (59) THE FLOOD, the protagonist now wisely checks his advance, though without becoming completely immobile. A forward impetus remains, as was the case in TÚN (3) GATHERING SUPPORT.

Notes

1. RESTRAINT — The word 節 *jié* basically refers to a section of the trunk of a bamboo. Because each section is a closed cylinder, the word came to mean "limit" or "restraint."

2. "door" (first line), "gate" (line two) — In a Chinese house compound, several buildings are contained within a wall. The "door" is the entrance to one of the buildings. The "gate" is the entrance to the compound as a whole.

3. "strict restraint" (line five) — See also LÍN (19) LEADERSHIP, line three.

61

忠孚　ZHŌNG FÚ

WHOLEHEARTED ALLEGIANCE

Wholehearted allegiance.
Piglet and fish are auspicious.
It is favorable to cross a great river.
It is favorable to keep on.

It is better to be a faithful and lowly subject than to seek independence. The help of a strong ruler will make it possible to succeed in such great undertakings as crossing a dangerous ford. Piglets and fishes were offerings given to the spirits by people of low rank, where noblemen offered sheep or even oxen.[1]

Lines

first line/9 —— It is auspicious to be prepared.
Unexpected disquiet lies ahead.

The weak subject represented by this lowest line can prepare for danger by joining a strong ruler.

line two/9 —— A crane calls from the shade
And its chick answers.
"I have a fine goblet."
"I will partake with you."

The mother crane is like a ruler and the crane chick her subject. The goblet symbolizes official rank and its benefits. Shade symbolizes protection. Line two is the place of the subject, who responds to his ruler's offer of protection and rank.

line three/6 — — Enemy captives:
                 Some are vigorous and some exhausted.
                 Some weep and some sing.

Line three is almost always inauspicious. The least auspicious way of becoming the subject of someone strong is to be taken by him as a prisoner.

line four/6 — — The moon comes full.
                 A horse runs away.
                   No harm.

Though the horse runs away, it will return again, like the full moon.

line five/9 —— Bound by allegiance,
                 He comes to no harm.

The subject's loyalty to his ruler protects him from harm. Line five is the place of the ruler.

top line/9 —— A cock flies to the sky.
                Keeping on will bring misfortune.

It is unnatural for a cock to fly so high. The highest line of a hexagram often shows someone who goes too high, bringing himself into conflict with someone stronger.[2]

STRUCTURE ☴ 巽 Xùn   Kneel in Submission
           ☱ 兌 Duì   Stand Straight (break free)
The word 忠 *zhōng* "wholehearted" is closely related to the word 中 *zhōng* "middle," "center." In the center of this hexagram is a pair of weak lines (☷), held between pairs of strong lines (☰) above and below them.

SEQUENCE   In the previous hexagram JIÉ (60) RESTRAINT, a subject had to restrain himself from advancing too quickly. In WHOLEHEARTED ALLEGIANCE, he restrains himself from seeking independence and remains a loyal subject of his ruler.

Notes

1. WHOLEHEARTED — The word 忠 *zhōng* "wholehearted" is really the same word as 中 *zhōng* "middle." In ancient times, both were written as 中.

2. "cock" (top line) — The word 翰音 *hànyīn* "cock" refers specifically to the cock used in certain sacrifices. The protected crane chick of line two has become a sacrificial cock. The evil omen of the flying cock is reminiscent of an incident during the reign of the great Shang king *Wǔdīng* 武丁. While the king was preparing to offer sacrifice, a cock-pheasant flew up and lighted on the handle of a *dǐng* ritual caldron. This was interpreted as a warning from the royal ancestors that the dynasty was going to fall. (書經 *Classic of Documents*, 高宗肜日 "The Day of Wuding's Sacrifice" section.)

62

小過　XIǍO GUÒ

SMALL GETS BY

Small gets by.
Blessed.
It is favorable to continue.
One may do small things but not great.
The bird that flies will leave only a cry,
It should not be on high but down below.
Then it would have great good fortune.

Attempt only small things, do not strive too high. The bird that exposes itself in the air will be shot down. The bird that remains hidden in the bushes will be safe.[1]

Lines

first line/6 — —　　The bird that flies
　　　　　　　　　Will suffer misfortune.

Stay in the low position represented by this lowest line. Do not take the beginning of the hexagram as the beginning of a high flight.

line two/6 — —　　He passes by his grandfather,
　　　　　　　　　But meets his grandmother.
　　　　　　　　　He does not reach the lord,
　　　　　　　　　But meets the servant.
　　　　　　　　　He comes to no harm.

In each of these two cases, he humbly seeks out the lesser of two partners, thereby avoiding harm. Line two is the place of the subordinate, the woman, the servant.[1, 2]

line three/9 ——— Be careful not to go too far
Lest you be attacked.
Inauspicious.

Line three is the place of danger. Here at the top of the lower trigram one is in danger of rising too high or going too far. The phrasing of the Chinese suggests that the attack may come from behind.

line four/9 ——— No harm.
Not pass but encounter.
There is danger ahead, be on guard.
Do not keep right on as you are.

It is all right to keep on advancing as long as you prepare yourself for a dangerous encounter that lies ahead. In this fourth line, you successfully cross the barrier into the upper trigram, but not without difficulty.[1, 2]

line five/6 —— Dense clouds but no rain
From our western lands.
The duke shoots
And takes the bird from its hole.

He pulls back in time from his dangerous ambitions, is plucked from obscurity by the ruler and given high rank. Line five is the place of the ruler. Rain symbolizes conflict. The clouds of excess ambition build, but dissipate before they bring a rain of conflict.[3, 4]

top line/6 —— He passes by without encounter.
The bird that flies is netted.
Misfortune.
This means disaster.

He goes too far and is destroyed. Like other peoples, including North American Indians, the Chinese used to catch birds by stringing large nets across their flight paths.[1, 2]

STRUCTURE ☳ 震 Zhèn Thunderbolt (rush forward)
☶ 艮 Gēn Keep Still (stopped)

One keeps still in a low position (lower trigram ☶) rather than rushing forward into a high one (upper trigram ☳). The two solid lines in the middle of the hexagram are seen as passing across the gap between the lower and the upper trigram (═). In the hexagram DÀ GUÒ (28) BIG GETS BY, four solid lines pass that gap (≡).

SEQUENCE   The last hexagram ZHŌNG FÚ (61) WHOLE-HEARTED ALLEGIANCE showed a loyal subject resisting the temptation to seek independence. SMALL GETS BY shows him having success by not trying to exceed his present position.

Notes

1. GETS BY (title), "passes" (line two, line four, top line) — All these translate the same word 過 guò.

2. "meet" (line two), "encounter" (line four, top line) — These translate the same word 遇 yù.

3. "Dense clouds but no rain" (line five) — See also the opening text of XIĂO XÙ (9) SMALL IS TAMED.

4. "shoots" (line five) — The word 弋 yì "shoot" refers to shooting with an arrow to which a string has been attached, so that the arrow and the game it pierces can easily be retrieved.

63

☵ 既濟

JÌ JÌ

ALREADY ACROSS

Already across the ford.
Blessed.
Small should remain as he is.
Beginning: auspicious.
Ending: disarray.

One series of events has finished and another series is about to begin. Only small actions or beginnings are auspicious. Greater actions and endings are beyond one's power. Fording a river symbolizes any uncertain and dangerous undertaking or chain of events.[1]

Lines

first line/9 —— The wheels of his carriage drag in the mud.
The little fox gets his tail wet.
No harm.

Such difficulties are not dangerous here at the beginning of the crossing. Later on in the deeper waters at midstream, they could be disastrous. There the weight of the fox's tail would pull him under and the immobilized carriage would be exposed to enemy arrows.[2, 3]

line two/6 — — A wife loses her carriage curtain.
She must not chase after it.
In seven days she will get it back.

As long as she remains passive (— —), someone will make good her loss. Line two is the place of the subject, who loses the protection of a ruler, then gains it back.[4]

line three/9 —— When High Ancestor attacked the Land of Gui,
It took him three years to conquer it.
A little man must not take action.

Line three is associated with difficulty and danger. The task that
presents itself here is beyond the ability of anyone less than a great
lord.[5, 6]

line four/6 —— His padded jacket gets wet.
He remains apprehensive all day.

Fording a river, he wades out into water deep enough to get his
jacket wet, then either stops or proceeds only with great and sus-
tained caution. In line four he has advanced into the upper trigram.
This trigram Kǎn ☵ Pit sometimes represents a river. See RÚ (5)
GETTING WET.[7]

line five/9 —— The Eastern Neighbor slaughters an ox,
But this does not bring as full a blessing
As the Western Neighbor's modest offering.

One succeeds by doing only small things. The Zhou lived in the west
and their Shang overlords lived in the east. Not only could the Zhou
not afford such huge offerings to the spirits as were made by Shang,
but they considered their frugality a virtue. Line five is the place of
the ruler and of success.[8]

top line/6 —— He gets his head wet.
Danger.

He wades out into water that is too deep for him. The top line of a
hexagram is associated with going too far and with conflict.[9]

STRUCTURE ☵ 坎 Kǎn   Pit (danger)
             ☲ 離 Luó   Shining Light (shining, shone
                         upon)
One shines or is shone upon in a low or early position (lower trigram
☲), but encounters danger in a high or more advanced one
(upper trigram ☵). It is therefore better to remain low. The upper
trigram Kǎn ☵ Pit represents a river to be forded.

SEQUENCE   The protagonist of the hexagram has survived the
change of regimes that took place in GÉ (49) REVOLUTION and
DǏNG (50) THE RITUAL CALDRON and has found a place in the
new regime. This is the river he has forded. Now a new river of

greater achievement lies before him—perhaps the achievement of high position in the new regime, perhaps a revolution and establishment of his own regime. For the moment, however, he is advised not to step too far into the stream, to attempt no great deeds.

Notes

1. ALREADY ACROSS — See next hexagram WÈI JÌ (64) NOT YET ACROSS, especially the Sequence section.

2. "in the mud" (first line) — The original text says only: "His wheels drag." "Carriage" and "mud" are supplied from context. See line three of both RÚ (5) GETTING WET and KUÍ (38) ESTRANGEMENT and line two of NOT YET ACROSS.

3. "fox" (first line) — The original text says only: "Gets his tail wet." That this refers to a fox is inferred from the opening text of NOT YET ACROSS.

4. "carriage curtain" (line two) — This curtain may be above the rider for protection from the sun or around her for protection from the eyes of others.

5. "High Ancestor" (line three) — High Ancestor (高宗 *Gāo Zōng*) is a title of the great Shang king *Wǔdīng* 武丁 , who reigned about two hundred years before the Zhou conquest of Shang. This reference to a great Shang king is one tenuous indication that the *Changes* may have its roots in Shang times. See also NOT YET ACROSS, line four, and ZHŌNG FÚ (61) WHOLEHEARTED ALLEGIANCE, note 2.

6. "Gui" (line three) — "The Land of Gui" (鬼方 *Guǐfāng*) was the home of a northwest border tribe that was attacked and defeated by Zhou warriors on behalf of Shang. To call a country a 方 *fāng* ("direction," "place") is characteristic of the language of Shang and is therefore another possible indication of an early date for at least this part of the *Changes*. See also KUÍ (38) ESTRANGEMENT, top line.

7. "padded jacket" (line four) — The words 衣絮 *yī rú* probably refer to a coat or jacket padded with silk or cotton wadding, similar to those worn in China today.

8. "modest offering" (line five) — The word 禴 *yuè* is said to refer to the summer offering, which was small because the grain in the fields was not yet high enough to harvest. The same word is translated "small offering" in the second lines of both CUÌ (45) GATHERING AROUND and SHĒNG (46) RISING.

9. "gets his head wet" (top line) — See also the top lines of both DÀ GUÒ (28) BIG GETS BY and NOT YET ACROSS.

64

WÈI JÌ

NOT YET ACROSS

Not yet across.
Blessed.
Unfavorable for the little fox:
   He gets his tail wet
   just before he reaches the shore.

One is in midstream on a dangerous ford. Success is certain for all but someone small and weak, who will drown before reaching the shore. This "little fox" gets his showy tail wet and it drags him under. Fording a river symbolizes any uncertain and dangerous sequence of events.[1, 2]

Lines

first line/6 — —   He gets his tail wet.
                 Trouble.

When he is in deep water midway across the ford, the little fox's bushy tail gets wet and begins to drag him under. He should not have come so far. The weak line (— —) at the bottom of the hexagram symbolizes someone small and weak. This bottom line of the trigram Kǎn ☵ Pit is almost always inauspicious, especially at the bottom of a hexagram.[2]

line two/9 ——   His wheels drag.
               Keeping on will bring good fortune.

The wheels of his carriage drag in the mud of the river bottom, but he is still able to forge ahead. His horses will pull the carriage free.

This is an active line (——) in the place of the subject, who is aided by his ruler.[3]

line three/6 — —   Not yet across.
                   It is inauspicious to march to war,
                   But favorable to undertake the crossing of a
                       great river.

As long as his advance is peaceful and not aggressive, he will succeed. Line three is usually inauspicious. This inauspiciousness is mitigated here, perhaps by the fact that the line's being at midstream in the hexagram accords so well with the hexagram's overall meaning.

line four/9 ——   Keeping on brings good fortune.
                   Regrets will pass.
                   When the Thunderer attacked the Land of Gui,
                   In three years he had a reward from the Great
                       Nation.

Though it takes great effort, he will succeed. The "Great Nation" is Shang. The "Thunderer" probably refers to the Zhou ancestor who fought for Shang against Gui. This is said to have been Duke Jili 周公季歷 , the father of King Wen.   Line four is the place of the officer.[4, 5, 6]

line five/6 — —   Keeping on brings good fortune.
                   No regrets.
                   When the lord is glorious,
                   It is auspicious to bear him allegiance.

Loyalty to the ruler ensures success. Line five is the place of the ruler. The passive line (— —) suggests passive acceptance of the ruler's authority. The upper trigram Luó ☲ Shining Light symbolizes a glorious ruler.

top line/9 ——   Allegiance to someone who drinks.
                      No harm.
                   But if he gets his head wet,
                      Allegiance will miss the mark.

It is all right to bear allegiance to a ruler who goes a bit too far, but not to one who completely breaks the bounds of proper conduct. That the Shang drank too much was one of the accusations that the

Zhou used to justify rebellion. The top line of a hexagram often has to do with going too far and with conflict between subject and ruler.

STRUCTURE ☲ 離 Luó   Shining Light (shining, shone upon)

☵ 坎 Kǎn   Pit (difficulties, a river)

He is in the midst of difficulties (lower trigram ☵), but allegiance to a shining ruler will get him through (upper trigram ☲).

SEQUENCE   The protagonist of the previous hexagram JÌ JÌ (63) ALREADY ACROSS had completed the crossing of one river, but was not ready to start across another. The protagonist of NOT YET ACROSS is in midstream. Whether the two hexagrams refer to the same person and the same river is unclear. Perhaps ALREADY ACROSS shows someone who has found a place in the new regime and NOT YET ACROSS shows him improving that place. Perhaps ALREADY ACROSS shows someone who can hope for nothing better under the present regime and prepares to cross the river toward rebellion. In that case, NOT YET ACROSS shows someone else who can indeed hope for higher position even under the present regime. In either case, the *Changes* does not end statically. Its protagonist is in motion, not yet at the end of the present movement of his fate.

Notes

1. NOT YET ACROSS — Compare with JÌ JÌ (63) ALREADY ACROSS.

2. "gets his tail wet" (opening text and first line) — See also ALREADY ACROSS.

3. "his wheels drag" (line two) — See also line three of KUÍ (38) ESTRANGEMENT and the first line of ALREADY ACROSS.

4. "the Thunderer" (line four) — This line can also be read: "Like a thunderbolt we attacked the land of Gui and in three years had a reward from the Great Nation."

5. "the Land of Gui" (line four) — See line three and note 6 of ALREADY ACROSS.

6. "the Great Nation" (line four) — During the early years of the Zhou Dynasty, Shang was still referred to as the Great Nation. Use of such an expression is one of the things that suggests an early Zhou date for at least part of the *Changes*.

APPENDICES

APPENDICES

APPENDIX A
The Sequence of the Hexagrams

QIÁN (1) STRONG ACTION ☰ Active principle. A strong person appears and takes action.

KŪN (2) ACQUIESCENCE ☷ Passive principle. He should become the subordinate of someone greater.

TÚN (3) GATHERING SUPPORT ☵☳ He must restrain himself and gather support before advancing to enter the ruler's service.

MÉNG (4) THE YOUNG SHOOT ☶☵ He does not restrain himself, but advances recklessly. Fortunately, someone else restrains him.

RÚ (5) GETTING WET ☵☰ He is now strong enough to brave difficulties and go to join the ruler.

SÒNG (6) GRIEVANCE ☰☵ He complains to his ruler that he is not being given opportunities for advancement.

SHĪ (7) AN ARMY ☷☵ He earns advancement by fighting in his ruler's army.

BǏ (8) ALLIANCE ☵☷ His allegiance to the ruler protects him from harm.

XIǍO XÙ (9) SMALL IS TAMED ☴☰ He advances too quickly, but restrains himself in time to avoid conflict with the ruler.

LǙ (10) TREADING ☰☱ He advances too far, offending against the ruler, but his offense is forgiven.

TÀI (11) FLOWING ☰ He makes a smooth, strong advance with his ruler's help.

PǏ (12) BLOCKED ☷ His ruler blocks his advance.

TÓNG RÉN (13) WITH OTHERS ☰ He advances in company with others, not alone.

DÀ YǑU (14) GREAT WEALTH ☰ He has wealth to buy his ruler's favor and is enabled to advance.

QIÀN (15) MODESTY ☷ He is strong enough to advance into high position, but modestly refrains.

YÙ (16) CONTENTMENT ☷ He is strong enough to become a leader, but too content as he is to make the effort.

SUÍ (17) THE HUNT ☷ He goes out and wins merit.

GǓ (18) ILLNESS ☶ He retreats to his home to care for his sick father.

LÍN (19) LEADERSHIP ☷ He rises from below to assume a minor position of leadership.

GUĀN (20) WATCHING ☴ He stops to observe his situation, remaining a subordinate rather than advancing into a danger-ously high position.

SHÍ HÈ (21) BITING THROUGH ☲ By determined action, he wins through to a shining prize.

BÌ (22) ADORNED ☶ The shining prize he has won makes him attractive to his ruler.

PŌ (23) DESTRUCTION ☶ He sets himself too high and is cut down.

FÙ (24) RETURN ☷ He retreats in time to avoid this destruction.

WÚ WÀNG (25) NO EXPECTATIONS ☰ He abandons his ambitions and good fortune comes to him.

DÀ XÙ (26) BIG IS TAMED ☶ He allows himself to be tamed and put to use by his ruler.

YÍ (27) BULGING CHEEKS ☶ Having "fed" to the point that his cheeks bulge, he stops to digest his gains so that his bulging cheeks will not attract attack.

DÀ GUÒ (28) BIG GETS BY ☰ He has gone too far to stop and must forge ahead.

KĂN (29) PITS ☵ He advances and falls into difficulties, but will be rescued by his ruler.

LUÓ (30) SHINING LIGHT ☲ His shining ruler nurtures him.

GĂN (31) MOVEMENT ☶ He begins to move again, after having been stopped by his fall into difficulties.

HÉNG (32) CONSTANCY ☳ Though once again active, he is careful not to attempt to raise his status.

TÚN (33) THE PIGLET ☰ Like a piglet, he accepts confinement and grows bigger.

DÀ QIÁNG (34) BIG USES FORCE ☰ Like a charging ram, he grows big enough to burst free of his confinement.

JÌN (35) ADVANCEMENT ☷ He is granted advancement by his ruler.

MÍNG ZHÌ (36) THE BRIGHT PHEASANT ☷ He is a brilliant minister whose ruler will not listen to his advice.

JIĀ RÉN (37) THE HOUSEHOLD ☴ Despite some dissatisfaction, he remains an obedient member of his ruler's household.

KUÍ (38) ESTRANGEMENT ☲ His estrangement increases and he leaves his ruler's service.

JIĂN (39) STUMBLING ☵ On his own, he runs into difficulties.

XIÈ (40) GETTING FREE ☵ He extricates himself from difficulties by withdrawing.

SŬN (41) REDUCTION ☶ Only by reducing himself from independence to a subordinate position is he enabled to advance.

YÌ (42) INCREASE ☴ He advances quickly, doing great deeds in his ruler's service.

JUÉ (43) FLIGHT ☱ His ruler orders him to stop, but he keeps rushing forward and runs away.

GÒU (44) SUBJUGATED ☴ He does not run away, but stops and is subjugated.

CUÌ (45) GATHERING AROUND ☱ Rather than being subjugated, he freely rallies to his ruler's service.

SHĒNG (46) RISING ☷☴ He rises in his ruler's service.

KÙN (47) BURDENED ☱☵ He is granted high position in the service of his ruler, but his high position is a burden to him because of the ruler's failings.

JǏNG (48) THE WELL ☵☴ He realizes that the ruler is not nourishing his people and that he himself would do better.

GÉ (49) REVOLUTION ☱☲ He overthrows the ruler.

DǏNG (50) THE RITUAL CALDRON ☲☴ He establishes a new regime.

ZHÈN (51) THUNDERBOLTS ☳☳ A vassal of the deposed ruler quakes with terror as the conquerors strike like thunderbolts.

GÈN (52) KEEP STILL ☶☶ The vassal keeps still and out of harm's way.

JIÀN (53) GRADUAL ADVANCE ☴☶ He moves gradually toward union with the conqueror.

GUĪ MÈI (54) A MAIDEN MARRIES ☳☱ He joins the conqueror humbly, like a lowly concubine, and is able to rise to high status.

FĒNG (55) ABUNDANCE ☳☲ He finds a place in the glorious new order.

LǙ (56) THE WANDERER ☲☶ He continues to seek his proper place in the new order.

XÙN (57) KNEELING IN SUBMISSION ☴☴ He has no alternative but to kneel to the conqueror.

DUÌ (58) STAND STRAIGHT ☱☱ He rises from his knees to his feet.

HUÀN (59) THE FLOOD ☴☵ He is swept off his feet by the ruler's power, but ends up in an unexpectedly high position.

JIÉ (60) RESTRAINT ☵☱ He restrains himself from seeking a dangerous advance.

ZHŌNG FÚ (61) WHOLEHEARTED ALLEGIANCE ☴☱ He remains a loyal subject of the ruler and does not seek independence.

XIǍO GUÒ (62) SMALL GETS BY ☳☶ He succeeds by remaining small and doing only small things.

JÌ JÌ (63) ALREADY ACROSS ䷾ He has forded the river of finding a place in the new regime. Now a new river of achievement lies before him, which he must not enter too boldly.

WÈI JÌ (64) NOT YET ACROSS ䷿ He has not yet reached the far shore of the river he is fording. Greater achievement is possible to him if he keeps on.

APPENDIX B
Divination in Ancient China

There were two main methods of divination in ancient China: oracle bone divination and yarrow divination. The earlier and more respected of these was oracle bone divination, which was the method used by the Shang kings. The *Changes* is a handbook of yarrow divination.

In oracle bone divination, diviners read omens from the shape of the cracks that appeared when a piece of shell or bone was heated with a burning stick or a red-hot poker. The stiff stalks of the common yarrow or milfoil plant were used in yarrow divination. Diviners took their omens from a hexagram constructed on the basis of random manipulations of a bunch of about fifty of these stalks.

Oracle bone divination Shang diviners normally used either the belly shell of certain species of tortoises or the shoulder blade of an ox. They prepared it by polishing one side and carving rows of centimeter-long dimples into the other. To make a divination, the red-hot poker was applied to the edge of one of the dimples. The omen was read in the cracks that sprouted on the polished side of the bone or shell. These consisted of a crack along the length of the dimple with a spur or spurs to one or both sides, e.g., ├ , Қ , ᚺ, ┼ . No one knows how the diviner read omens from these cracks.

After a divination had been made, it was recorded in an inscription on the actual piece of bone or shell used. When all the space on a bone or shell had been used up, it was placed in the royal archives underground. Thousands of inscribed pieces of bone and shell have now been found in the ruins of the Shang capital.

The inscriptions record divinations on a wide variety of subjects: sacrifice, war, the hunt, journeys, banquets, the harvest, official reports, eclipses, sun, rain, snow, illness, death, the birth of a child, dreams, the coming week, and even the coming afternoon. Most inscriptions record the date of the divination (by the 60-day Chinese calendrical cycle), some record the name of the diviner, some record his judgment, and a few record what actually happened, as well.

Here are some examples:

> Day 55, diviner Gu divines: If we hunt at Qiu, will we make a catch? On this day's hunt, we actually caught 1 tiger, 40 deer, 164 foxes, and 159 elk.
>
> Day 8, diviner Zheng divines: What will happen if Fuhao joins Zhijia and they attack the land of Ba?
>
> We divine offering a pig to Father One (one of the Shang ancestors, each of whom was associated with a day of the ten-day week).
>
> Offering 100 dogs and 100 oxen?
>
> Will there be rain in the fifth month?
>
> Divination: The king hunts. Will he go and come back without misfortune?
>
> Will we not encounter wind?
>
> Will the king's week be without misfortune?
>
> We divine ordering Lord Chuan of the Clan of the Many Princes to attack Zhou.
>
> Shall we take in the millet harvest?
>
> Shall we not take in the harvest?
>
> Auspicious.
>
> Very auspicious.

Yarrow divination Since the tortoises used were rare and valuable, oracle bone divination was a very expensive method, the use of which was reserved to only the wealthiest lords. Yarrow divination may have arisen as a cheaper alternative, perhaps among the common people, perhaps in the Zhou homeland on the distant western frontier of the Shang empire. Yarrow divination is also easier than oracle bone divination. In fact, the word 易 *yì* can mean "easy" as well as "change." It is quite possible that the *Changes* should really be called the *Easy*.

The earliest hints of the existence of yarrow divination are found on oracle bones dated to the time of the Shang king Wuding, around 1250 B.C. On these bones are inscribed series of six numbers that are now believed to represent the six lines of hexagrams.[1]

The first literary mention of yarrow divination comes in the *Classic of Documents* (書經 *Shūjīng*) in a section that may have been written as early as Western Zhou (circa 1000–750 B.C.). The Duke of Zhou tells his fellow regent the Duke of Zhao not to resent being subordinate to the young King Cheng, whom their deceased brother

King Wu had appointed as his successor, breaking the Shang custom of brother succeeding brother. He explains the importance of subordinates to the health of the state, drawing examples from the great days of Shang:

> So Heaven gave full blessings to Shang and established the laws, which the common people and the king's men all strove to follow, the lesser knights, the great lords, and most of all the king's close associates. Thus did virtue rise as they assisted their superiors. One man had servants in the four quarters of the world and whether he divined by tortoise or by yarrow the answer was that all bore him true allegiance.[2]

There is no indication of the details of yarrow divination until the divinations recounted in the *Zuo Commentary* (左傳 *Zuŏzhuàn*), a history of the Spring and Autumn Period (750–500 B.C.) that was written during the Warring States Period (500–250 B.C.). The first direct and detailed description of how to go about selecting a hexagram appears in one of the *Ten Wings* commentaries on the *Changes* that was probably not written until late Warring States or early Han (circa 300–100 B.C.).

If the *Changes* was in fact written during Western Zhou and Spring and Autumn, as I suspect, then we have no direct way of knowing how it was used by the diviners who wrote it. Late as it is, however, the information we do have gives us some idea of how the *Changes* was used in ancient times. Some details are given in Appendix C.

As many as fourteen divinations are recounted in various versions of the *Zuo Commentary.* Of these, three are on the future of a newborn son; two are on whether or not to attack someone; two are on whether or not to go to someone's rescue; and there are one each on which of two sons to make one's heir; on whether to marry a certain woman; on whether to give a daughter in marriage; on whether to rebel; on whether to enter a lord's service; and on one's general situation.

The simplest kind of interpretation is based directly on the literal meaning of the divination text quoted.

> At dawn, the armies of [the southern state of] Chu approached the armies of Jin and arrayed themselves in battle formation. Bihuang of Miao said to the Duke of Jin: "Chu's best troops are those of the royal clan, in the center of their line. If you divide them by attacking on the

left and right flanks and then concentrate all three of
your main armies in the center of the line, you will certainly win a great victory." The duke made divination of
this plan and the diviner said: "Auspicious. The hexagram is FÙ [24, RETURN] which says, 'The southern
nation approaches. Its king is shot in the eye.' The nation
approaches and its king is harmed. How can it avoid
defeat?" [574 B.C.][3]

This is one of the cases in which a quote given in the *Zuo Commentary* does not appear in our version of the *Changes*. It may come
from another version; it may come from another divination book
now lost; it may have been devised by the diviner on the spot; and it
may be the entirely spurious invention of the author of the *Zuo
Commentary*.

Sometimes the literal meaning of the divination text bears no
apparent relation to the question asked and special knowledge of the
Changes' symbolism is required to interpret it.

When Nankuai was going to rebel against the Duke of
Lu, he made divination and received KŪN [2 ☷ AC-
QUIESCENCE] changing to BǏ [8 ☷ ALLIANCE].
This says: "Yellow skirt. Supremely auspicious." [The
text of line five of ACQUIESCENCE.] He considered it a
very good omen and showed it to Zifu Huibo, asking him,
"What does this mean if I intend to take action?" Huibo
replied, "This is something I have studied. It means that
if what you intend to do is something loyal and faithful
you may go ahead, but if it is not you will be defeated. The
outside is hard and the inside is gentle—this is loyalty.
[The lower or "inner" trigram of ALLIANCE is ☷ ,
which is composed entirely of passive or "gentle" lines.
The upper or "outer" trigram has a solid or "hard" line in
the middle ☵ . The upper trigram represents the ruler,
the lower the subject.] Harmony follows steadfastly—this
is to be faithful. [The lower trigram Kūn ☷ Acquiescent remains steadfastly the same in both hexagrams.]
That is why it says, 'Yellow skirt. Supremely auspicious.'
Yellow is the color of the center. The skirt is the lower
adornment. Supreme is the highest good. If the center is
not loyal, it does not merit its color. If what is below does
not contribute to what is above, it is not an adornment. If
what is done is not good, it cannot be the highest good.
Harmony between outer and inner is loyalty. Acting with

faithfulness is making a contribution. Nourishing the three virtues is goodness. Without all of these things, the divination does not apply. The *Changes* cannot be used to divine something improper. What is it you plan that it will be an adornment? If the center is fine, it can be yellow. If what is above is fine, it can be supreme. If what is below is fine, it is the skirt. If all three are there, the divination may be followed. If even one is lacking, though the omen be auspicious, it may not." [529 B.C.][4]

This divination makes clear a very important principle in using the *Changes*. The lines cannot be applied mechanically: Their relationship to the question must be established before an interpretation is made. A line that says loyalty brings good fortune cannot be used to justify rebellion just because it contains the words "good fortune." Zifu Huibo applies this line in the same way that I would, though he arrives at his interpretation in what seems a convoluted way. See line five of KŪN (2) ACQUIESCENCE in the translation.

A number of divinations in the *Zuo Commentary* associate the various trigrams with such things as parts of the body, natural forces, and family relationships. These associations are not used to establish the basic outlines of the answer but to flesh it out with more detail and to explain why the text of a certain line reads as it does.

When his son Jingzhong was little, Duke Li of Chen had a visiting diviner from the state of Zhou divine about him, using the *Changes of Zhou*. The hexagram was GUĀN [20 ䷓ WATCHING] changing to PǏ [12 ䷋ BLOCKED] and the diviner said: "This says, 'Behold the nation's glory. It is good to be a guest of its king.' [The text of line four of WATCHING, by changing which WATCHING is changed to BLOCKED.] This means that he will succeed Chen and rule a nation, but in another country, not here, and not he himself, but his descendant. 'Glory' means that his light will shine far. The trigram Kūn ☷ is earth; the trigram Xùn ☴ is wind; the trigram Qián ☰ is Heaven. Wind becomes Heaven, over earth [☴ over ☷ becomes ☰ over ☷]. This refers to a mountain. He has the mass of a mountain and shines with Heaven's light over the earth. This is why it says, 'Behold the nation's glory.' His courtyard is filled with a hundred travelers, who give him gifts of jade and silk and all the beautiful objects of the world. Therefore it says, 'It is good to be a guest of its king.'

There is still something to behold, so it means that all this will happen later. The wind ☴ moves over the earth ☷ , so it will happen in another country. If it is in another country, it will probably be in the country of the Jiang. [Chen's giant eastern neighbor Qi was ruled by a branch of the Jiang 姜 clan.] Jiang is behind the mountains and the mountains are companions of Heaven. Two things cannot be great at the same time, so he will not flourish until Chen declines." When Chen was first subjugated by Chu, Chen Huan became an important man in Qi. After Chen was finally destroyed by Chu, Chen Chengzi became ruler of Qi. [671 B.C.][5]

Most of the identifications of trigrams with natural forces, etc., are foreign to the text of the *Changes*, but they became important elements of *Changes* interpretation throughout the history of traditional China.

No matter where or how it is practiced, divination has always been used simply to confirm a decision that has actually already been made. Some of the Shang oracle bone divinations appear to have been repeated until the desired answer was obtained. There is also evidence of wishful thinking in some divinations made with the *Changes*:

Tang Jiang, the wife of Duke Tang of Qi, was Dongguo Yan's elder sister. Yan was a retainer of Cui Wuzi and when Duke Tang died it was he who drove Cui to pay his last respects. When Cui saw Tang Jiang, he thought her beautiful and ordered Yan to get her for him as his wife. But Yan objected. "A man and wife must be of different families. You, my lord, are of the Ding clan and I and my sister are of the Huan [both of which were branches of the royal family of Qi]. Such a marriage is not permitted." Cui made divination and got KŪN [47 ䷜ BUR-DENED] changing to DÀ GUÒ [28 ䷛ BIG GETS BY]. The diviners all said this was auspicious, but when he showed it to Chen Wenzi, Wenzi said, "Husband ☴ follows wind ☴ and wind harms a wife. You must not marry her. Moreover the text of the [changing] line says, 'Weighed down by boulders, he leans for support on thorns. He enters his palace and his wife is not there.' [This is the text of line three of BURDENED]. 'Weighed down by boulders' means that if he advances he will not reach his goal. 'Leans for support on thorns' means that what he loves is harmful. 'He enters his palace and his wife is not there' means that he will have nowhere to go home to." Cui said, "She is a widow, what harm could there be in it? All of this refers to her previous husband." So he married her. [When the new duke made love to Tang Jiang, Cui killed him and set up another man as duke, with himself as chief minister. He was later forced to commit suicide by self-strangulation and his whole family was executed.] [547 B.C.][6]

Unless the diviners mentioned here were simply introduced as a dramatic element in the story, it is evident from this passage that some diviners succumbed to the temptation of sycophancy. It is inconceivable that they could honestly have interpreted the divination as approving Cui's marriage to Tang Jiang.

Notes

1. See Zhang Yachu (1982).

2. *Classic of Documents*, "Order to Zhao" (Zhāo Hào 召公) section.

3. *Zuo Commentary*, 16th year of Duke Cheng (成公), quoted in Gao (1963), page 122.

4. *Zuo Commentary*, 12th year of Duke Zhao (昭公), quoted in Gao (1963), page 123.

5. *Zuo Commentary*, 22nd year of Duke Zhuang (壯公), quoted in Gao (1963), page 123.

6. *Zuo Commentary*, 25th year of Duke Xiang (襄公), quoted in Gao (1963), page 124.

APPENDIX C
Divination with the *Changes*

One of the best ways to learn to understand the *Changes* is to use it in divination. Without this, the ancients' attitudes toward it must always remain partly hidden. I myself, however, no longer use it in this way.

This is not because I do not think it works. My own experience suggests that it does work—how I am not sure. It usually gave me answers that seemed significant and it answered one important question in exactly the same way on three separate occasions. And it accurately predicted an event would happen "in ten years." But rather than allow the *Changes* to make my decisions for me, it seemed better to make them myself. Rather than develop an addiction to knowledge of the future, it seemed better to accept what fate brings.

The ancient Shang apparently believed that the spirits of their ancestors spoke to them through the oracle bone divinations. The early Zhou probably believed that the answers to their divination questions were given by Heaven, the supreme deity. Later Chinese and modern Westerners usually ascribe the answers to the mysterious power of the book itself. Carl Jung, in his famous preface to Richard Wilhelm's translation of the *Classic of Change*, suggested that significant answers appear because of "synchronicity," which he described as "an acausal connecting principle" reflecting "the peculiar interdependence of objective events among themselves, as well as with the subjective (psychic) states of the observer." It is also possible that the *Changes* is so framed that almost any hexagram will provide an apparently significant answer to almost any question.

But unless we do so a priori, we cannot exclude the possibility that the answers may in fact be provided by spirits, as the most ancient Chinese believed. Christianity and many schools of Buddhism consider contact with such spirits inadvisable or dangerous. Of course, it is more reasonable to think that apparently supernatural phenomena are either illusory or that they are actually manifestations of one's own unconscious psyche. This does not make them any less powerful.

On the other hand, many people in the English-speaking world use the *Changes* often and see no danger in it, but only benefit. Not only can it help in making advantageous decisions and teach a kind of humility in the face of circumstances, but in the process of interpreting the answers one can learn a great deal about one's own nature.

Jung thought that the *Changes* works in part by giving us new ways of looking at our problems. In trying to see a situation in the terms suggested by a divination, we explore our unconscious understanding. The book, he wrote, "represents one long admonition to careful scrutiny of one's character, attitude, and motives."

How to Make a Divination There are three stages in making a divination: asking the question, randomly choosing a hexagram to answer it, and interpreting the answering hexagram.

Asking the question It is important to ask the right question and to ask it in the right way. The *Changes* is best adapted to answering three types of questions. The first type proposes a certain action, such as attacking another state, getting married, or taking a job. The second asks what will happen during a particular period of time, such as the next week, month, or year. The third kind asks the *Changes* to tell about a certain person. These three types can be combined, for instance by asking what will happen to a certain person over a certain period of time or if one gets married at one time as opposed to another.

Do not ask either/or questions such as "Should I advance or retreat?" Ask two separate questions and compare the answers.

And do not ask vaguely, "What should I do?" Either propose a specific course of action or ask the *Changes* to describe your present situation. In doing so, it will suggest how best to act.

A useful form for questions is: "(Someone) divines (something)." For example: "Mary divines her coming year," "John divines going home." This is one of the forms used in the *Zuo Commentary*. The other is: "What if (someone does something)?" For example: "What if I make my second son my heir?"

Before making a divination, it is important to be in a serious and receptive frame of mind. Only with a calm and open mind is it possible to avoid the pitfalls of seeing only the answer you want or the one you fear, rather than the one that is actually given.

Selecting the hexagram *Changes* divination began in antiquity as a form of yarrow divination. The answering hexagram was cast by counting out groups of the stiff stalks of the common yarrow plant. During the Tang and Song dynasties (about 600–1300 A.D.), a simpler method using coins became popular. More recently, an American student of the *Changes* has devised an even simpler method that reproduces the statistical patterns of the yarrow method, which the coin method does not.

Whichever method is used, it will yield a set of six numbers, one for each line of the hexagram. Each one of these numbers will be a 6, a 7, an 8, or a 9. These four numbers stand for the four possible types of lines:

6	broken changing to solid	— →	———
7	solid	———	
8	broken	— —	
9	solid changing to broken	——→	— —

Starting at the bottom of the hexagram, one number is selected for each of its six lines.

When all six lines are unchanging 7's or 8's, the hexagram formed is itself the divination, e.g.:

```
8    — —    KÙN (47) BURDENED. Blessed. It is auspicious for a
7    ———              big man to persevere, he will
7    ———              come to no harm. Words
8    — —              spoken against him will not
7    ———              be believed.
8    — —
```

When one line is a changing 6 or 9, that line is the divination, e.g.:

```
8    — —    BURDENED
7    ———
9    ——→    line four: He moves slowly, bogged down in a bronze
8    — —              carriage. His difficulties will have an end.
7    ———
8    — —
```

When more than one line is a 6 or a 9, a second hexagram is formed by changing those lines and the two hexagrams together are the answer to the divination, e.g.:

KÙN (47)	8	— —	— —	HUÀN (59)
BURDENED	7	——	——	THE FLOOD
Blessed. It is auspi-	9	——→	— —	Swept by a flood.
cious for a big man	6	— →	——	Blessed. A king calls
to persevere, he will	7	——	——	down blessings to
come to no harm.	8	— —	— —	this temple. It is

Words spoken against him will not be believed.

favorable to cross a great river. It is favorable to persevere.

Usually the first situation is seen as changing into the second.

The yarrow method It is best to use actual yarrow stalks, prefer-ably about a foot or so long, but thin wooden rods like chopsticks can also be used and even toothpicks will do in a pinch.

preliminary step: Start with 50 sticks. Set one aside to make 49.

bottom line:

A.1 — Divide the 49 sticks at random into two bundles.

A.2 — Remove a stick from one of the two bundles and set it aside.

A.3 — Count through each bundle by fours.
Set aside the last group of 1 to 4 sticks from each bundle.
Combine the two bundles.
The combined bundles will total 44 or 40 sticks.

B.1 — Divide the 44 or 40 sticks at random into two bundles.

B.2 — Remove a stick from one bundle, as in A.2.

B.3 — Count through, set aside, and combine, as in A.3.
The total will now be 40, 36, or 32 sticks.

C.1 — Divide the remaining 40, 36, or 32 sticks at random, as in A.1 or B.1.

C.2 — Remove a stick, as in A.2 or B.2.

C.3 — Count through, set aside and combine, as in A.3 or B.3.
The total will now be 36, 32, 28, or 24 sticks.

D — Divide the remaining 36, 32, 28, or 24 sticks into bundles of four sticks each.
There will be 9, 8, 7, or 6 bundles, respectively.
Write this number down for the bottom line of the hexagram.

line two: Repeat steps A–D.
line three: Repeat steps A–D.
line four: Repeat steps A–D.
line five: Repeat steps A–D.
top line: Repeat steps A–D.

The advantage (and disadvantage) of the yarrow method is the amount of time it takes. The complexity of the operation makes divination a serious process and helps to clear and concentrate the mind.

The procedure described here, long and complicated as it is, is slightly simpler than the traditional one described in other translations. Both are based on Chapter 9 of the *Appended Judgments* (繫辭 *Xìcí*), one of the *Ten Wings*. The traditional procedure follows an interpretation of that chapter by the Song Dynasty philosopher *Zhū Xī* 朱熹 ; I follow a reinterpretation by Gao (1963) and Chen (1972).

The coin method This simple method has been popular since the Tang and Song dynasties (600–1300 A.D.). It is the method commonly used in the West today:

1. Use three coins. Chinese copper coins are available in many Chinese curio shops.
2. Throw them all three together like dice, once for each line of the hexagram, starting with the bottom line.
3. Tails (inscribed side of a Chinese coin) = 2.
   Heads (uninscribed side or side with less writing) = 3.
4. three tails = 2 + 2 + 2 = 6
   two tails, one heads = 2 + 2 + 3 = 7
   two heads, one tails = 3 + 3 + 2 = 8
   three heads = 3 + 3 + 3 = 9
5. Repeat once for each line of the hexagram.

The method of sixteen This is a new and even simpler method proposed by Schoenholtz (1975). Its main advantage is a statistical one. With the yarrow method, the probabilities of getting each of the four different kinds of lines are not the same: the chances of getting a broken line (8 — —) are 7 out of 16; the chances of getting a solid line (7 ——) are 5 out of 16; for a solid line that changes (9 ——→), they are 3 out of 16; and for a broken line that changes (6 — →), there is only 1 chance in 16.

With the coin method, on the other hand, the chances of getting either kind of stable line are 6 out of 16 and those of getting either kind of changing line are 2 out of 16.

The method of sixteen reproduces the probabilities of the yarrow stalk method. The new method uses 16 small objects such as beads, shells, or pebbles, all the same size and shape but of four different colors or patterns: 7 of one color or pattern, 5 of another, 3 of another, and 1 of another. Each of the four groups represents a different kind of line: 7/16 = 8 — —, 5/16 = 7 ——, 3/16 = 9 ——→, 1/16 = 6 — →. Blindly choose one of these objects for each line, putting it back with the others before choosing again for the next line. I myself used small shells placed in a cloth bag.

The answering hexagram Whichever method you use, you will end up with a hexagram that may have one or more changing lines. Use the table on page 238 to find out what hexagram it is, then turn to the translation and commentary for that hexagram.

1. If it has no changing lines, the hexagram as a whole is the divination. Read its opening text and the Structure and Sequence sections. The individual lines can be read as aids to understanding, but they do not specifically apply. Questioners often make the mistake of giving too much importance to a line that does not properly apply to their situation, but which they find appropriate or attractive.

2. If there is one changing line, then that line is the divination. Take your answer from its text and commentary. Read about the other lines and the hexagram as a whole only in order to understand the significant line better.

3. If there are two or more changing lines, change them to form a second hexagram. The two hexagrams together are your answer. Normally, the situation symbolized by the first hexagram is seen as changing into that symbolized by the second, but the two can be related in other ways as well. Take your divination from the hexagrams' opening texts and Sequence and Structure sections. The individual lines do not apply, but can be read to help you understand the hexagrams.

Ancient divination techniques Ancient diviners, at least as represented in the *Zuo Commentary* and *Conversations of the States* (國 語 *Guóyǔ*) histories, may have used a slightly more complex method of deciding what to take as their divination. Gao (1963) and Chen (1972) have suggested that some 6 — → and 9 ——→ lines were not allowed to change.

Add together the six numbers that represent the six lines of the answering hexagram. Subtract this from fifty-five, which is the sum of all the numbers from one to ten. Take the remainder and count upward from the bottom of the hexagram by that number of lines. If the number is more than six, count the top line twice. The line at which the count ends is the only one that is allowed to change, e.g.:

```
6    — →            6 7
6    — →         5     8
7    ——       4       9
7    ——    3          10
8    — —  2              11      14
7    ——  1                   12 13
 —
```

55 − 41 = 14

In the example, FĒNG (55) ABUNDANCE, only line two is allowed to change. Since it is not a changing line, it does not change. Even though there are two changing 6 — → lines in the example, they do not change and the hexagram as a whole is the divination.

On the other hand, if there are three or more moving 6 — → or 9 —→ lines, they all change when the count falls on a stable line. When the count falls on one of the moving lines, only that one line changes.

In addition to this complex procedure, Gao and/or Chen discovered that when three lines change, the divination comes from both the original and the new hexagram. When more than three lines change, the divination comes mainly from the new hexagram, with a sort of shading from the original. There are no examples in ancient literature of two lines changing, but it is reasonable to expect that in that case the divination would come mainly from the original hexagram, with shading from the new.

The recent discovery of hexagram notations from Shang and early Zhou presents an entirely new field of study. These notations include numbers such as 5 and 1 that were not used even in the mid and late Zhou divinations considered by Gao and Chen. No one has yet presented a complete hypothesis of how these earliest divinations were made.

Interpreting the answer This is the most important, interesting, and difficult part of making a divination. The diviner's role is crucial. The *Changes* never provides a simple "auspicious" or "inauspicious." A line or hexagram symbolizes a situation; its text describes that situation, says whether it is auspicious, inauspicious, or something in between, and sometimes recommends a course of action. It is up to the diviner to decide what is the parallel between the answering hexagram and his question.   For a simple example, the text of the hexagram BĬ (8) ALLIANCE says: "Alliance is auspicious." If the question was "Shall I get married?" the answer would probably be "Yes." If the question was "Shall we get a divorce?" the answer would probably be "No."

The diviner must take into account not only the question itself but all the circumstances surrounding it. For example, the question "I divine marrying N," answered by the hexagram XÙN (57) KNEELING IN SUBMISSION, the text of which reads: "Kneeling in submission. Small is blessed. It is favorable to go forward. It is favorable to go to see someone big." This suggests that marriage is a good idea, but only if you can somehow see yourself as the weaker partner going to marry the stronger. Perhaps it means you should marry someone other than N. Perhaps it accurately describe's N's submission to you. Perhaps it helps you realize that you are in fact the weaker partner.

The hexagram is a metaphor of the situation about which the question asks. Reason and intuition work together to find the relationship between the two. The diviner devises logical ways of applying the hexagram to the question and one of them intuitively clicks. Or he or she intuitively feels a relationship and tests it by studying the hexagram more carefully. The process is not always quick. The answer may be misty and indistinct at first, but it will gradually become clearer.

Although the general meaning of the hexagram is more important than any single image in the text, sometimes a phrase or image will stand out, giving such a clear and apposite answer that it can't be ignored. Even in such cases, it is still best to read and understand the hexagram or line in detail to confirm, qualify, or erase the initial impression. Not that everything in the text of a line or hexagram must apply in every situation. The *Changes* is a collection of diviners' notes, guidelines to what the hexagrams and lines mean in various situations.

Sometimes an answer will stubbornly remain unintelligible. Be very slow to give up on it. In order for the *Changes* to be effective, the answers it gives should always be considered correct. The diviner may not understand an answer because he unconsciously rejects the advice he is getting. Or the *Changes* may be answering a question that is more important than the one directly asked.

The *Changes* gives its answers in terms of an ancient society. This can be disconcerting and sometimes difficult to relate to modern conditions. But people aren't really so different; the relationships the *Changes* speaks of are deeply rooted in our psyches.

The *Changes* is inescapably hierarchical. The placement of the lines one above the other is the basis of its symbolism. Ruler and subject, big man and little man, high position and low position are fundamental categories in the text. This is socially undesirable in our egalitarian age, but not actually alien to the ways in which we treat one another. At any given time in any relationship, one partner can be regarded as leading or dominant.

Women are seen in two ways in the *Changes*. On the one hand, their place is in the home, supporting their husbands. On the other hand, a "woman" is often a metaphor for a ruler who is receptive to a subject's desire to join him (her). In each divination, the diviner must decide whether to take reference to a woman literally or as referring to someone (female or male) who acts in a womanlike way.

Frequent references to war in the *Changes* are confusing and annoying to some people. In our own lives, we seldom ask questions directly concerned with war. But it is not hard to find metaphorical battles in business, love, sports, politics, and even writing. The *Changes'* world is a harsh one and we must be prepared to hear warnings of conflict or misfortune expressed in the most vivid and uncompromising terms.

The *Changes* as a whole depicts its protagonist's rise to power through cycles of alliance and conflict. This is a path of desire and self-aggrandizement, but also a path of growth. Throughout the *Changes*, what is auspicious is what leads ultimately to growth. The protagonist alternates periods of protected growth as an obedient servant with periods of active growth, sometimes involving war.

An important thing to remember about *Changes* divination is that its verdicts are not immutable. When the *Changes* says that trouble lies ahead, it at the same time advises retreat. By changing what you do, you can change the future.

APPENDIX D
Chinese Pronunciation

The transliteration system employed in this book is the *Hànyŭ Pīnyīn* 汉語拼音 system used in the People's Republic of China and now becoming common in newspapers and among scholars. Neither of the systems in general use—*Hànyŭ Pīnyīn* or Wade-Giles—gives English speakers easy access to Chinese pronunciation. For those who would like to make a stab at correct pronunciation, the following approximate equivalents may be useful:

a = *a* as in p*a*rt
ai = *i* as in al*i*ve
ao = *ou* as in *ou*ch
e = *e* as in *a*lert
ei = *a* as in f*a*de
i (normally) = *ee* as in f*ee*l
i (after s, sh, c, ch, z, zh, r) = a light buzzing sound represented in one transliteration system by an *r* (e.g., chr) or a *z* (e.g., sz).
ie = *ye* as in *ye*t
ian = *yen*
iu = *yo* as in *yo*lk
o = *o* as in p*o*rt
ou = *o* as in l*o*pe
u (normally) = *oo* as in l*oo*p
u (after j, q, x) = ü
ü = French u or German ü (round your lips to say "oo" but say "ee" instead)
ui = *way*
un = *won*
ue = *we* as in *we*t

c = ts
z = dz
zh = j
q = ch (used before i or ü sounds)
x = sh (used before i or ü sounds)

Other sounds are much as in English.

APPENDIX E
Chronology of Early Chinese History

STONE AGE (circa 600,000 B.C.–circa 2000 B.C.)
    Palaeolithic period begins about 600,000 B.C.
    Neolithic period begins about 7000 B.C.
SHANG DYNASTY (circa 1750 B.C.–circa 1000 B.C.)
    Traditionally said to begin 1766 B.C. Other estimates
        1700–1500 B.C.
ZHOU DYNASTY (circa 1000 B.C.–256 B.C.)
    Traditionally said to begin 1122 B.C. Other estimates 1066 B.C.,
        1027 B.C.
    Western Zhou circa 1000 B.C.–771 B.C.
    Eastern Zhou 771 B.C.–256 B.C.:
        Spring and Autumn period 722 B.C.–481 B.C.
        Warring States period 403 B.C.–221 B.C.
QIN DYNASTY (221 B.C.–206 B.C.)
HAN DYNASTY (206 B.C.–220 A.D.):
    Western Han 206 B.C.–9 A.D.
    Eastern Han 25 A.D.–220 A.D.

SELECTED
BIBLIOGRAPHY

In English

BLOFELD, John. *I ching*. London: George Allen and Unwin (1965)

CHANG Cheng-lang 张政烺. "An interpretation of the divinatory inscriptions on early Chou bronzes." First published *Kaogu Xuebao* 考古学报 1980.4. English translation *Early China* 6 (1981)

CHANG Kwang-chih 張光直. *Shang civilization*. New Haven: Yale University Press (1980)

CHEN Shih-chuan 程石泉 (Cheng Shiquan). "How to form a hexagram and consult the I Ching." *Journal of the American Oriental Society, v.* 92, no. 2 (1972)

DOERINGER, F. M. "Oracle and symbol in the redaction of the I Ching." *Philosophy East and West* 30, pp. 195–209 (1980)

DOUGLAS, Alfred. *The oracle of change*. London: Gollancz (1971)

GERNET, Jacques. *Ancient China*. First published in French 1964. English translation London: Faber and Faber (1968)

HSU Chin-hsiung 許進雄 and Alfred Ward. *Ancient Chinese society*. South San Francisco: Yee Wen (1984)

KEIGHTLEY, David N. "The Shang state as seen in the oracle bone inscriptions." *Early China* 5 (1980)

KEIGHTLEY, David N. *Sources of Shang history*. Berkeley: University of California Press (1978)

LEGGE, James. *I ching*. First published 1882. New York: University Books (1964)

LOEWE, Michael. "Manuscripts found recently in China." *T'oung Pao* 63, pp. 99–136 (1977)

NEEDHAM, Joseph and WANG LING 王玲. "The system of the Book of Changes." In *Science and Civilisation in China*, v. 2, pp. 304–45. Cambridge University Press (1956)

SCHOENHOLTZ, Larry. *New Directions in the I Ching*. Secaucus, N.J.: University Books (1975)

SHCHUTSKII, Iulian K. *Researches on the I Ching*. First published in Russian 1960. Princeton University Press (1979)

WATSON, William. *Early civilisation in China*. London: Thames and Hudson (1966)

WILHELM, Hellmut. *The Book of Changes in the Western tradition—a selective bibliography*. Seattle: Institute for Comparative and Foreign Area Studies, University of Washington (1975)

WILHELM, Richard. *The I Ching or Book of Changes*. First published in German 1924. English translation 1950. Princeton University Press (1967)

WING, R. L. *The illustrated I Ching*. Garden City, N.Y.: Doubleday (1982)

ZHANG Yachu 长亚初 and LIU Yu 刘雨. "Some observations about milfoil divination based on Shang and Zhou *bagua* numerical symbols." First published in Chinese *Kaogu* 考古 1981.2. English translation *Early China* 7 (1982)

In Oriental Languages

AN Jinhuai 安金槐. "Henan Xia-Shang wenhua de xin shouhu 何南夏商文化的新收获." *Wenwu* 文物 1983.3

GAO Heng 高亨. *Zhou Yi dazhuan jinzhu* 周易大传今注. *Jinan:* Qi-Lu Shushe 齐鲁书社 (1979)

GAO Heng. *Zhou Yi gujing jinzhu* 周易古經今注. Shanghai: Kaiming Shudian 開明書店 (1947)

GAO Heng. *Zhou Yi gujing tongshuo* 周易古經通說. First published Peking 1958. Hong Kong: Zhonghua Shuju 中華書局 (1963)

GU Jiegang 顧頡剛 ed. *Gushi bian* 古史辨, v.3. First published Peiping 1931. Hong Kong: Taiping Shuju 太平書局 (1962)

GU Jiegang. "Zhou Yi guayaoci zhong de gushi 周易卦爻辭中的故事." In GU ed. (1962)

GUO Moruo 郭沫若. *Zhou Yi de goucheng shidai* 周易的購成時代. Shanghai: Commercial Press (1940)

HONDA Wataru 本田济. *Ekigaku* 易学. Tokyo: Heirakuji Shoten 平樂寺書店 (1960)

LI Hansan 李漢三 . *Zhou Yi guayaoci shi yi* 周易卦爻辭釋義 .
    Taipei: Zhonghua Congshu Bianshen Weiyuanhui 中華叢書編
    審委員會 (1969)

LI Jingchi 李鏡池 . "Yi zhuan tanyuan 易傳探源 ." In GU ed. (1962)

LI Jingchi. "Zhou Yi shici kao 周易筮辭考 ." In GU ed. (1962)

LI Jingchi. *Zhou Yi tanyuan* 周易探源 . Peking: Zhonghua Shuju 中
    华书局 (1978)

LI Jingchi. "Zhou Yi shici xukao 周易筮辭續考 . First published
    1947. In LI (1978)

Mawang Dui Han Mu Boshu Zhenli Xiaozu 馬王堆汉墓帛书整理小
    組 . "Mawang Dui "Liushisi Gua" shiwen 馬王堆《六十四卦》
    釋文 ." *Wenwu* 文物 1984.3

QU Wanli 屈萬理 . "Shuo Yi sangao 說易散稿 ." *Wen-shi-zhe
    Xuebao* 文史哲學報 7 (1956)

QU Wanli. "Zhou Yi guayaoci cheng yu Zhou Wu Wang kao 周易
    卦爻辭成於周武王考 ." *Wen-shi-zhe Xue-bao* 1 (1950)

RONG Chaozu 容肇祖 . "Zhanbu de yuanliu 占卜的源流 ." In GU
    ed. (1962)

RWAN Yuan 阮元 ed. *Zhou Yi zhushu* 周易注疏 . First published
    1815. Reprint Taipei: Xuesheng Shuju 學生書局 (1967)

WANG Kaifu 王開府 . "Zhou Yi jing-zhuan zhuzuo wenti chutan
    周易經傳著作問題初探 ." *Kong-Meng Yuekan* 孔孟月刊 ,
    v. 10, no. 10 (1961)

XIE Dahuang 謝大荒 . *Yi Jing yujie* 易經語解 . Taipei: Yuandong
    Tushu Gongsi 遠東圖書公司 (1959)

XU Qinting 徐芹庭 . *Zhou Yi yiwen kao* 周易異文考 . Hong Kong:
    Shijie Tushu Gongsi 世界圖書公司 (1975)

XU Shida 徐世大 . *Zhou Yi chanwei* 周易闡微 . Hong Kong:
    Taiping Shuju 太平書局 (1962)

YAN Lingfeng 嚴靈峯 . *Yixue xinlun* 易學新論 . Taipei: Zheng-
    zhong Shuju 正中書局 (1969)

LOWER TRIGRAM \ UPPER TRIGRAM	Qián	Kūn	Kǎn	Luó	Zhèn	Gēn	Xùn	Duì
Qián	1	11	5	14	34	26	9	43
Kūn	12	2	8	35	16	23	20	45
Kǎn	6	7	29	64	40	4	59	47
Luó	13	36	63	30	55	22	37	49
Zhèn	25	24	3	21	51	27	42	17
Gēn	33	15	39	56	62	52	53	31
Xùn	44	46	48	50	32	18	57	28
Duì	10	19	60	38	54	41	61	58